TALES FROM THE DYKE SIDE

by Jorjet Harper

Illustrations by Michèle Marie Bonnarens

with Christine Steiner

TALES FROM THE DYKE SIDE

by Jorjet Harper

Illustrations by Michèle Marie Bonnarens

with Christine Steiner

New Victoria Publishers

Published by New Victoria Publishers Inc., a feminist, literary and cultural organization. PO Box 27, Norwich, VT 05055-0027

Back Cover Photo by Toni Armstrong Jr.
Illustrations © Michèle Marie Bonnarens

Printed and bound in Canada
1 2 3 4 5 6 2000 1999 1998 1997 1996

Library of Congress Cataloging-in-Publication Data

Harper, Jorjet, 1947-
Tales from the dyke side : essays / Jorjet Harper
p. cm.
ISBN 0934678-71-5
1. Lesbianism--United States. 2. Gays in popular culture--United States. I Title.
HQ75.6.U5H38 1996
306.76'63--dc20

95-52018
CIP

For Ma and Mary

Contents

Introdyktion

When my first book, *Lesbomania,* came out in 1994, the review I most appreciated was from the *Bay Area Reporter*. Deborah Peifer wrote: "Jorjet Harper reminds us, with superb writing and delightful wit, that the reason to be a lesbian is for the sheer joy of it." Naturally I was very pleased by that statement. I do think that being a lesbian is the greatest thing since the invention of the wheel, and that was exactly what I was hoping to convey in the pieces in that collection.

Of course the "superb writing and delightful wit" comment was gratifying, too.

Like the wheel, however, lesbians seem to find ourselves being reinvented over and over again. It can get disturbingly dizzying at times. And sometimes, surrounded by confusion and bombarded by hateful muck, we have to make an active effort to seek out the happier aspects of being a lesbian. Nevertheless, "for the sheer joy of it" will always, to my mind, be the very best reason to be a dyke—and the best reason to be alive.

What I hope to convey in *Tales from the Dyke Side* is that to be a lesbian in our modern world is to be in a unique, sometimes marvelous, sometimes scary, but never-dull position from which to observe the panorama of society at large. Despite homophobia and other constraints on lesbian and gay lives, I thank my lucky stars that fate, or my environment, or genes, or hormones, or courage, or common sense, or everything put together graced me with the good fortune to be a lesbian during this lifetime.

Lesbians continue to develop our self-definitions, arts, culture, and political strength, and that alone is very exciting. As the media "discover" us, new intersections become visible across mainstream popular culture—including art, entertainment, science, religion, and politics—and lesbian, gay, and queer culture. At this point, lesbian images often still teeter between invisibility and distortion. But rich veins of humor, meaning, and clarification about all sorts of things outcrop from these sharp, dynamic cultural shifts. *Tales from the Dyke Side* is the result of my most recent field expeditions.

Is there a dyke "side" to anything? Working for years at a lesbian and gay newspaper where we were admonished to look for a lesbian angle in practically every subject we covered, from wine tasting to missile testing, I must say I was surprised to discover that distinctly lesbian perspectives exist in even the most unlikely arenas, and that undoubtedly there is at least one dyke side to almost any topic you can think of.

Once in awhile it even feels as if there's a parallel dyke universe that also exists in a different dimension entirely.

At the very least, being a lesbian in a world-assumed-to-be-heterosexual often requires leaps from one context to another, to jump across the gaps in those everyday assumptions—about sex, identity, culture, behavior, desire, loyalties, families, intentions, goals—and arrive at a new way of looking at something that includes and affirms lesbian realities. Leaping from one context to another is exactly what humor requires, too. Which is maybe why humor writing seems so well-suited to my thinking.

Now, I grant that I can't always tell if I have a "different" perspective on something because I'm a lesbian, or because I'm just a quirky sort of person. But to me, a lot of the unimaginative social assumptions and behaviors that constitute many people's projections of "normalcy" are just as strange, exotic, unhealthy, and ultimately false in the cosmic scheme of things as any of the bent things straight people have imagined about lesbians.

Occasionally, presumptions about lesbian "positions" even from within queer culture are absurd. Some gay male conservative is arguing for "our" metaphorical "rightful place at the table" afforded by the traditional "family values" of American society? Who does he think he's gonna con into taking their "rightful place" in the metaphorical sweltering kitchen, where my mother and grandmother were stuck cooking, serving, washing the patriarchy's metaphorical dirty dishes, and dumping out the metaphorical garbage, while the male members of the traditional family valued their relaxation by imbibing traditional American intoxicants? Not me, dude, I'm metaphorically outta there.

It helps to recall that even the word "funny" itself was once a euphemism for queerness. "I think that fellow who runs the flower shop on Broadway is a little funny," my parents used to say. I find the entire world we live in to be a very "funny" place. Of course, ultimately I can only speak for myself, and hope that as I celebrate the growth of lesbian culture and lesbian creativity, my take on things resonates for others, even when they don't identify with my experiences or agree with my slant on things.

Since joy informs the very root of my feelings on the subject of lesbianism, I hope that *Tales from the Dyke Side*, like *Lesbomania*, conveys something of that joy to you. My own Dyke Side is the place where I can express my "funniest," most playful, most lesbian thoughts and experiences, and savor them. Living well may be, as they say, the best revenge, but it's not always an option. On the other hand, laughing well is certainly the best and most economical remedy for homophobia-induced frustration and depression. And loving well—well, gee, that's how I got into this lesbianism thing in the first place.

—Jorjet Harper
Chicago, March 1996

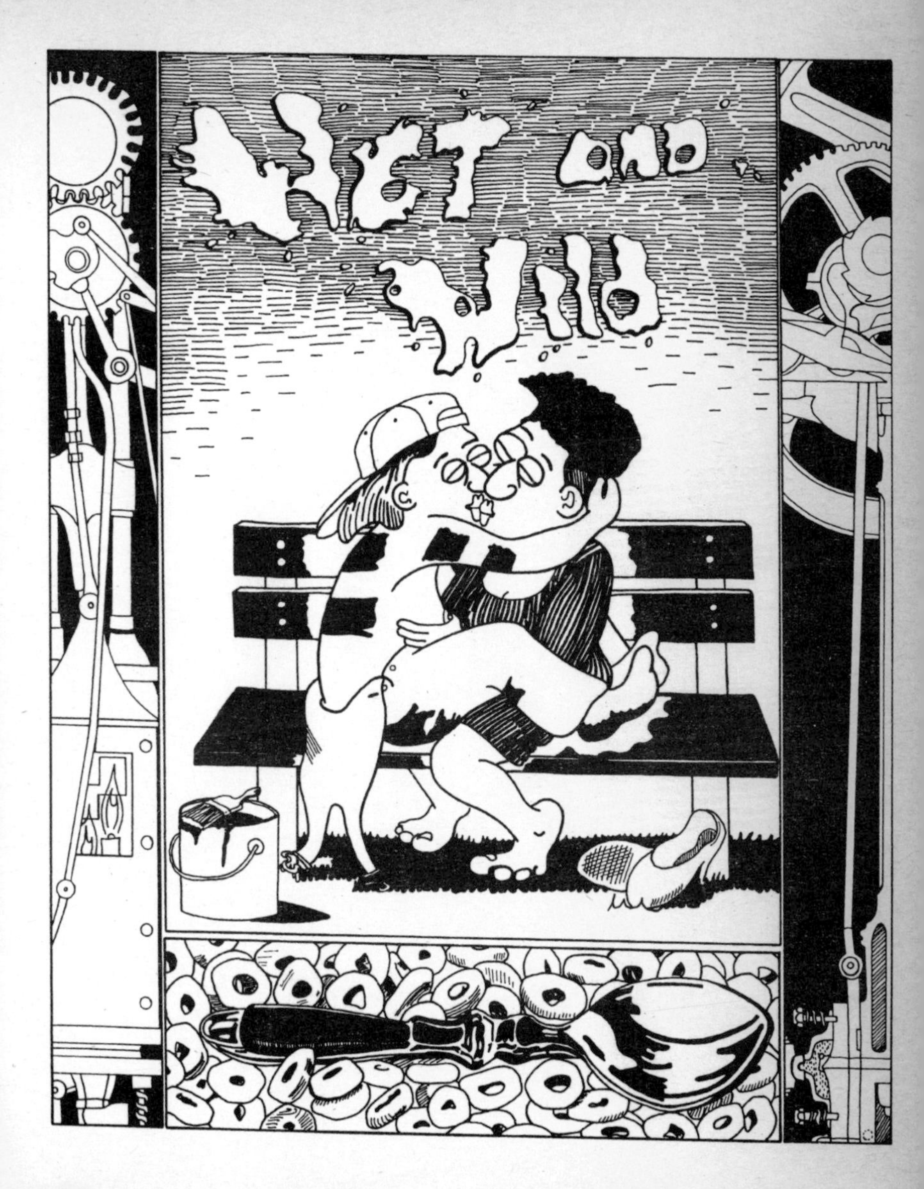
WET AND
Wild

For flavour, Instant Sex will never supersede the stuff you had to peel and cook.

—Quentin Crisp

Breakfast Cereal Monogamy

At first, you can't get enough of each other. Lust encircles both of you like the aroma of fresh brewed coffee—you can always go for another cup. Your first few times in bed it's Total and yummy. It's hot Cream of Wheat. It's flapjacks and country ham. Grits and gravy. She knows how to stir your emotions up into a porridge, and you know just how to quake 'er oats. You melt in each other's mouths.

For weeks or even months you keep cooking up a delicious, nutritious, steaming bowl of hot cereal monogamy together and it seems like life will be one long Power Breakfast after another.

Then after awhile, it becomes less hot but still satisfies. You look forward to the few times it's really juicy. You maybe stir in some smooth fresh peaches or firm ripe strawberries. But at some point the sex wilts into monotony, like routinely ordering the same kind of bagel and cream cheese over and over simply from habit.

And after a few years, your sex life together has lost every molecule of freshness—if and when you have it at all. It's turned into a tepid, congealed, unappetizing leftover that no longer has the slightest bit of snap, crackle, or pop. You might even feel queasy from a case of sexual indigestion.

Oh, certainly, you may still love her, still want to be with her. But lately she's got her nose buried not in you but in the newspaper, and there you are chewing awkwardly on some soppy shredded wheat that tastes like cardboard.

Face it: your libidos have flatlined, honey. Your sex life is toast.

This painful but inevitable state of affairs is neither your fault nor hers. No matter what romantic myths are perpetrated by mainstream culture, no matter how you try to deny it, the harsh truth is that eroticism in monogamous relationships has a finite shelf life.

And therefore I propose that in order to improve the situation and protect the rights of every consumer, the sexual activity of monogamous couples should, like all other perishables, have a clearly marked expiration date, conveniently located right on the package.

At the beginning of every love, we like to imagine that this one is going to be The One that lasts forever. But do you expect a box of Cheerios to last forever? Of course not. No matter how fortified it may be with vitamins and minerals, you know that eventually, like everything organic, it loses its freshness. Any good cook can tell you that. So why can't we admit that the same is true of our relationships, and act accordingly? It will save everybody a lot of grief just to see it right up front, stamped and official.

Now, I know that many lesbians have an aversion to being labeled. But it would be a public service to all involved if, after the first week of sleeping together, we took careful stock of each other and exchanged small notifications with a freshness warning, something like, "Best if used before JUN 1999..."

We'd expect at least that much from any reputable peanut butter and jelly manufacturer.

Why not stamp it right on the domestic partnership papers? At the expiration date, both partners can check it out carefully and see if it's still good. After all, sometimes a product can last quite a bit longer than the estimated expiration date—but then at least you know you're taking a chance.

How can anyone tell how long their current love life will stay fresh?

A good rule of thumb: for monogamous lesbian sex, figure around three years. Maybe a lot less, maybe even slightly more, depending on the ingredients.

When lesbians first get together, we often tell each other our sexual histories and past relationships. That should certainly give you both a big clue in accurately calculating the estimated shelf life of your mutual erotic hunger. But we often wait till things have gone rancid before we realize we should have noticed that "Sell by 8/10" sticker. We would have looked for it immediately if we were picking out a slab of bacon.

If you are already in the midst of a relationship, you know very well when you are bored and the freshness date is about to expire. You and your partner may try some stopgap measures. Special coupon offers, or little prizes in the box. You may check out a store like the Pleasure Chest, looking for a pick-me-up. Or you get sentimental, and do things together that are corny or flaky.

But eventually even these measures will be to no avail. And as we become more desperate, as our lust gets more and more dissipated, lacking in fiber, what do we tend to do about it?

We start processing more and more.

Big mistake. Processing may extend the apparent freshness date of your sex life, but it's really only acting as a preservative. No new nutrients are being pumped into the package, and processing often means injecting some really poisonous and dangerous additives.

But, you wail, we've already spent so much time together! What a shame to let it go to waste! How can we just throw what we have in the garbage!?

Think about that box of Raisin Bran that's been up in the kitchen cabinet for six years now. Do you want to keep it till it has mealy bugs? If something in the fridge or on the shelf has really turned moldy, you both know it's time to empty it out and go shopping.

It happens to everybody, if that's any consolation. It happens to straight people too, though it's harder to get a good estimate of the shelf life of straight sex since hets tend to deny reality longer—for the children's sake, for the relatives' sake, for the marriage's sake, for appearances…

At least if you're honest and aware that your hot lesbian sex is perishable, you won't feel guilty when you find yourself craving some tasty new sensation. You may not feel so desperate to pick up some hearty foreigner with an intriguing name like Gusielta Müesli. Or be tempted to break your sex fast with some fast sex by trying to get some cheap, greasy little McMuffin to stick to your ribs.

At the very least, an expiration date should help remind a couple that they'd better get the most out of their sex life together before it goes stale.

With the estimated sexual expiration date in mind, you can look at your cereal monogamy labels carefully before you go Post Toasties looking for Kix and Trix. Both of you can make a conscious decision about whether you've had enough, and whether or not you're ready to begin a new course.

One Little Difference

We were skeptical.

"No, really. I'm turning over a new leaf," Jenny said. "I've sown my wild oats, and I'm ready to settle down." She flashed her prettiest Julia Roberts smile. "I've found the One."

The One was a certain Janet, who lived in another state.

A few weeks later I got a printed invitation to the wedding, and there it was in black and white, even in calligraphy.

My friends and I sensed that the Marriage of Jenny to Janet was a historic event in the annals of Chicago lesbian sexuality. It was the end of an era. We had to see it with our own eyes.

Three of us—Mora, Barbara, and I—drove out together to the suburban banquet hall where the wedding and reception were being held. On the way, we speculated, as dykes often do before a lesbian wedding.

"What's your guess? Two brides, two grooms, or a mix?" said Barbara.

"Two brides," said Mora.

"One of each—Jenny bride, Janet groom," I said.

"Nah. Two grooms, I bet," said Barbara.

We were not referring to sex roles, but to whether the couple would both wear gowns, both wear tuxedos, or one dress and one tux. Lesbian wedding apparel, I've discovered, often defies the expected. Sometimes a very butchy woman will surprise everybody by walking down the aisle in a lacy dress, or someone you had pegged as the femmier half of the couple might don vest, tails and a top hat for this special occasion.

We waited behind another car for the longest time to make the turn into the parking lot, and we joked about the bad driver in front of us. Then it occurred to us that the bad driver must also be going to Jenny's wedding. When we all got out of our cars, we discovered that the bad driver was Ellen, Jenny's ex after Mora.

As we were about to enter the building, another woman arrived. I didn't know her, but Mora recognized her as someone who'd been sleeping with Jenny while Jenny was with Ellen.

Jenny and Janet greeted everyone inside. They were both wearing tuxedos with corsages on the lapels, and they both looked very nervous.

"Told you. Two grooms," said Barbara.

"So you're really going through with this!" I said to the bridal pair.

"Yup," said Jenny. She and Janet gazed at each other, cow-eyed.

Barbara and I got on line for a coke, and I found I was standing behind someone I hadn't seen in several years.

"Harriet," I said. "Nice to see you."

"Hi," said Harriet, smiling. "Nice to see you, too."

"I didn't know you knew Jenny."

"Well, I don't know her that well. But my lover Gina"—she pointed to a curly-haired woman who looked vaguely familiar—"She used to be lovers with Jenny."

That was why she looked familiar.

"I didn't know *you* knew Jenny, though," Harriet said.

"Oh yes, I've known her for years. And, well, actually, my lover Mora used to be lovers with Jenny."

"Oh," said Harriet. She looked a little confused.

"Mora was two or three after Gina, I think."

"Oh."

The three of us were impressed at how tactfully Jenny had arranged the seating. After scanning around the big reception room, we noticed that each of Jenny's ex-lovers had been placed at a different table, so nobody had to sit staring at their rivals or successors.

"It must have been quite a logistical project, figuring out how to do that."

"There may be even more, though, that we just don't know about."

"This is going remarkably well, all things considered." said

Mora.

It was true. But what impressed me more than the sterling behavior of Jenny's exes and her thoughtfulness in seating them was how well all Jenny and Janet's straight relatives were taking this lesbian union.

Both women came from large families. Siblings, uncles, nieces, nephews, some with their children along—lots of straight people, all taking a lesbian wedding completely seriously.

"As much as I think marriage is a crock of shit," I said, "I have to admit there's something touching about all this."

In fact, I'm embarrassed to admit it, but I tend to cry at lesbian weddings. It even brought tears to my eyes when I saw a front page picture in *The New York Times* of two young women getting their domestic partnership license at the City Clerk window in Manhattan. Just because we finally *could*.

"Yeah," said Mora. "Here's all of Jenny's family, and there's Janet's father—who looks like he's maybe a truckdriver, a regular guy—wearing a carnation in his lapel."

"He doesn't look exactly thrilled at the situation, but he's going along with it."

"Well, that's what makes gay weddings so important," said Barbara.

"What is?"

"You know how it is when lesbians read a book and we mentally change the pronouns? Or we watch a movie, and we have to adjust the genders in order to relate things to our own experience?"

"Of course I know. Those Star Wars movies, for instance. Once I started imagining Han Solo as a very tall woman in space cowboy drag, the love scenes with Princess Leia got interesting."

"Right. Well, that's just what these straight people have to do in this situation. It's a context they can understand. Everything looks like it should to them, except there's one little difference: it's two women instead of a man and a woman. It challenges their assumptions, but only so far—so they can accept them."

Barbara and I got up and wandered over to the big wedding cake. There were two little plastic grooms on top that really did resemble Jenny and Janet in their tuxedos.

"See what I mean?" said Barbara. "Just one small difference..."

The three of us had to offer our congratulations and make our goodbyes a little early, because we were headed off to yet another wedding that same afternoon. Two more of our lesbian friends were getting married, at a well-known Chicago jazz club.

"What do you think? Brides or grooms?"

The second wedding was even larger than the first, with family members flying in from all over the country. This time both women wore silk dresses and high heels. Judging by their clothes, I expected to see two miniature plastic brides at the apex of the huge tiered cake. Instead, they had two little figurines: a Pooh and a Piglet.

If Barbara's right, it's these little shifts that will eventually make all the difference in the world.

Taster's Choice

I confess I have never been to a lesbian orgy.

Okay, it's true that I've never been *invited* to a lesbian orgy, and for all I know most of the stories and rumors I've heard about such events have been highly exaggerated, or even made up for shock value.

Still, I don't doubt that a few of the group-grope super-hip parties women have talked about going to in Los Angeles really have happened. And I heard that for awhile there was a regularly scheduled lesbian orgy night somewhere in San Francisco. I don't know what went on at such parties in any detail, though I've heard a few rapturous accounts of multiple encounters, not knowing whose arm or leg or breast belonged to who, and so on.

What annoys me is that the few orgy-goers who have spoken up about these events tend to gloat. They act as if they have achieved the ultimate in one-up-woman-ship, hinting provocatively about their experiences, and implying that perhaps you who have not been to an orgy must be less courageous or maybe even simply non-orgy-asmic.

I haven't heard anyone brag about being to an orgy lately, though, so I don't know if they are still going strong or if it was a fad that has, so to speak, petered out.

But if, IF, I were ever invited to an orgy, I would undoubtedly choose not to go.

("If nominated, I will not run. If elected, I will not serve...")

That may sound like sour grapes, but I just don't get the attitude of so-called sex-positive lesbians who like to equate sexual "freedom"—and sexual excitement, for that matter—with fucking *strangers*. And imply that if you aren't willing to drop your jeans for any horny unwashed dyke who smiles and flicks a pubic hair in your direction, you are hopelessly stodgy, shockingly conservative, and you just aren't "with it."

Phooey.

Let's set the question of love aside for the moment and just talk about sex.

Why, I ask you, would I want to put my face, which I'm very attached to, between some stranger's legs? Lesbian or otherwise?

I want to know who she is first. Suppose it was someone I disliked? Someone who, say, unbeknownst to me, supports atmospheric nuclear testing? Or who I later discovered works as a furskinner for a company that clubs baby harp seals? Why would I want to be the agent of giving pleasure to such a person? And there's no way I'd enjoy being touched by a seal-killer, no matter how nice her nipples might be.

It's not that I *couldn't* do it. But aside from wondering if my anonymous partner was a nice person, I also know that having sex with a total stranger would be distasteful to me. I don't mean, like, in bad taste. I mean *distasteful.*

Allow me to speak quite plainly here. There's something about getting to know a woman, and discovering that I like her, and developing feelings for her, that makes her *taste good,* makes me want to kiss her, makes me like the smell of her skin, makes me know that her saliva—for starters—is something I will like having on my own tongue. Sometimes the process happens slowly, and sometimes I acquire a "taste" for a certain lesbian rather quickly. But always, I have to like someone quite a bit before I want to exchange bodily fluids. At the most basic level it's probably some chemical accumulation of pheromones or something like that.

But if sex doesn't feel good or taste good, what other reason is there to do it? Unless it's to prove something to somebody. Or to make a baby. And nobody has to have sex to make babies anymore.

I feel fine about my sexual predilections—or limitations, if you want to look at it that way. Call me stodgy if you must, but I don't want to eat out any random crotch any more than I want to suck on a slice of radiator hose. The fact that I have read in the newspaper that some people have actually eaten entire cars, tires and chrome and all, and lived to tell about it without even gastric distress doesn't make me feel that I'd better start crunching on the cylinder case of the nearest parked car if I want to stay "with it."

On the other hand, I'm willing to admit that people who can do such things may possess a skill I don't have. I *can't* eat a car. I don't even want to lick one square inch of leather auto upholstery. Similarly, I can't go muff diving with some random woman who might turn out to be Rush Limbaugh's wife without some time, however brief, to get to know her—to put it quaintly, courtship—and the more I like her, the more appealing she becomes.

I've noticed, while walking my little dog Spyke, that he can stick his nose a bare millimeter from just about *anything* with the same even expression of eager curiosity on his face. *Whiff whiff,* his tiny nostrils quiver, sucking in every molecule with nary a hint of negativity. No matter what it is. It's all new information for him. A big steamy pile of Doberman shit, a strange Schnauser's anus—he doesn't pull back unless it's a bucket of pure ammonia. He's not *stupid.*

On the other hand, Spyke has only actually had sex twice in his life, and both times he became a father. The religious right would give him its stamp of approval.

So, as tired as I am of being looked upon as a sexual fuddy-duddy by women who want to stick their curious noses everywhere, I'm equally tired of hearing people put down women who are promiscuous.

"Oh, she'll fuck anything that moves," I heard a dyke say just the other day, spoken in disparagement.

Is that *bad? Why* is that bad? Being able to fuck anything that moves is a talent that I think deserves some respect. Hey, can *you* do it? I sure can't. Even on multi-vitamins, five orgasms in one day has been my all-time personal best. Plus, fucking anything that moves must be at least as time-consuming as eating an automobile. Especially when there's a strong wind shaking the trees. Only the most dedicated could really succeed at such a thing.

I appreciate the outrageousness of sexually forward women. I don't see anything intrinsically wrong with having the ability to jump in and out of bed anywhere, anytime, if you really enjoy it. Assuming it's consensual. And so long as you gals who can fuck anything keep your roving eye off my cute innocent little dog.

I suppose that some women might have frequent semi-anonymous sex for reasons other than enjoying the sex itself. Like my junior high school friend Lynn who was always giving the boys a quickie, thinking that blow jobs in the back alley of the local hot dog stand was the best way to become "popular" in school.

She realized only much later that her logic had been totally phallacious.

Maybe some lesbians have other-than-sexual motives for going to orgies, too. Like looking for adventure. Or, this one-up-woman thing. Or to feel like they are on the cutting edge of sexual experience.

Myself, I tend to avoid the cutting edge because that's where you are most likely to get cut. And that's *definitely* not my thing.

Maybe a few lesbians go to orgies thinking they might find a nice girlfriend—and don't see why they should particularly start with the face. Good luck to them!

I think the only really nonsensical reason I've heard for going to an orgy is, as a lesbian who shall remain nameless said to me: "It made me feel attractive again."

Attractive!? Well, I was glad she had a good time, so I didn't want to nitpick about it—but what crossed my mind when she said that was, Who the hell would notice what you *look like* when bodies are anonymously sliding over each other, and somebody has their elbow between you and your current partner, and somebody else's foot is in your face?

But maybe looks count for a lot in these kinds of situations. According to gay friends of mine who remember the bathhouse days, looks were all-important there—and that's why they kept the lights real low in the bathhouse "orgy room," the last resort of those who hadn't found a partner elsewhere.

What you do sexually is your choice—just don't try to make me feel bad about my choices, okay? Live and let live, love and let love.

And don't bother to invite me to the orgy. Unless…would it be considered rude for a person to just stand around and take notes for a lesbian novel she's writing?

Promises, Promises

So many lesbians and gay men are getting married these days that you'd think it was legal!

If and when it does become legalized in the good old US of A, a rush of weddings will undoubtedly follow. Think of all the banquet people, caterers, ministers, tailors, florists, photographers—and eventually, lawyers—who are going to make a fortune from our long-denied craving for conventionality!

Once we have the option to marry we can make use of the services of legitimate marriage counselors specializing in marriage issues for real bona fide married people, too, not just the regular all-purpose kind of relationship counselors we rely on now.

Eventually we won't feel we need to get married just because we finally can. But for awhile I'm afraid we're likely to go overboard and try to out-family-value the traditionalists in our stampede to the altar.

So I've decided to hang out my own shingle as an Anti-Marriage counselor. I'm starting now because the rush of lemmings into the sea has already begun, judging from the number of gay and lesbian weddings I've been to just in the last year.

If you have any nagging doubts about taking the plunge, you can simply write to me for discouragement. If you have no doubt at all, you need my services even more. You'll wish you had consulted me when the (Pro) Marriage Counselors soak you for steep fees for three or four years before they advise you to divorce.

Dear Anti-Marriage Counselor,

I was once trapped in a heterosexual marriage and it was living hell. But now my lover says that if I marry her, things won't be like that at all, because it's two women. Is she right?

Wondering in Wooster

Dear Wondering,

If you took a poll of lesbians, I bet you'd find that those who were once married to men are the least enthusiastic about legalizing marriage between lesbians. Why would anyone in her right mind want to expose herself to that mental and emotional tyranny again, with just a change of the gender of her partner?

It's true that there may be some small differences if you "tied the knot" with a woman. Some lesbian couples might as well be married now. If you and your lover engage in conversations like: "Honey, did you wash my socks?""Yes, dear, they're in the top drawer," then why stop at marriage? Go all the way and get a lobotomy.

Dear Anti-Marriage Counselor,

If you think marriage is such a bad idea for everybody, how come you go to all these lesbian and gay weddings?

Scooter

Dear Scooter,

Despite my aversion to the institution of marriage, I support domestic partnership legislation and I believe that same-sex marriages should be legalized. I go to lesbian and gay weddings because I love my friends, I want to help them celebrate their happiness, and because lesbians and gay men are entitled to make the same stupid mistakes in our personal lives that straight people do.

Dear Anti-Marriage Counselor,

If we don't get married, what will prevent us from breaking up some day?

Dolly W.

Dear Dolly,

Nothing, if you're lucky. Generally when people maintain their own spaces or live together without getting married, they behave better toward each other. Since they don't have some ironclad contract, they know their partner always has the option to bail out if they aren't being treated well.

Doesn't it strike you as a noteworthy phenomenon that at the same time lesbian and gay male couples are pleading to get permanently glued together, straight people are filing for divorce left and right? Not *all* of those straight people are breaking up because they've discovered they're really gay.

Maybe some of those straight people know something we don't, for a change.

Dear Anti-Marriage Counselor,

I'm a deeply religious person and I dream of someday marrying my partner in a big church wedding with the blessings of the Holy Father.

Sr. Juana, San Antonio, Texas

Dream on, Sister. But consider your advantages: at least now nobody says you are living in sin because you aren't married. You're just living in sin because you're gay.

Dear Anti-Marriage Counselor,

I've found the woman I want to live with for the rest of my life.

Louisa May, Boston

Dear Louisa May,

The reason you want to live with this one woman for the rest of your life, and no other—even though you can't imagine where or what you will be doing, much less how long "the rest of" it will be—is because *the very institution of marriage has inculcated you with such a false sense of certainty!* Vowing to stay with someone forever is utter craziness. Nobody should promise anything FOREVER because nobody CAN promise anything forever. What if your partner becomes psychotic? Or is abusive? Or behind your back, runs up a gambling debt in Vegas on your credit cards? Why the hell should you stay with someone who turns out to be a jerk, just because you said you would?

Dear Anti-Marriage Counselor,

I need somebody around I can rely on to help raise my kids, and I'm not rich enough to hire a nanny.

Donna, Washington DC

Dear Donna,

I'm glad to see you're going into this with your eyes open. Does your future spouse know of your intentions, or are you the only pragmatist in the family?

Dear Anti-Marriage Counselor,

I don't see what your problem is. Marriage is something very special. If you marry someone, it means that they have a very special place in your heart that no one else can take.

Natalie in Pittsburgh

Dear Nat,

That's true. What you are saying, in effect, is, 'Darling, you're not in the same categories as all my other exes.' That's a great reason to swear eternal fidelity—to boost your girlfriend's ego. And when you do break up, you can hate each other so much more deeply than if you were just a couple, because you haven't just done each other wrong, you've ruined each other's lives!

Dear Anti-Marriage Counselor,

My sweetie and I have been together a long time, and we want the same rights and privileges straight couples have—legal benefits, medical benefits, social recognition...

Gertrude, Oakland, California

Dear Gert,

Women have *always* been pressured into marriage by the argument that it's to their social and economic advantage—and then they get sucked into all the assumptions about sex, about roles, about duties, and family obligations. Gay men and lesbians who marry will "improve" their marital status, all right, and the rest of us who don't marry will remain second-class citizens. *Everyone* should have access to adequate health care, no matter their age or marital status—don't you think? Why is it more "fair" if suddenly lesbian couples and gay male couples are able to take advantage of the already discriminatory rights that straight married couples have?

Dear Anti-Marriage Counselor,

Everybody else gets to do it so why shouldn't I?

Tanya, Portland, OR

Dear Tanya,

I don't have a good answer to that one, and that's the reason I advocate legalizing gay marriage. But I do recall that my mother said to me when I was a kid, "If everybody else jumped off the end of the pier, would you do it too?"

Dear Anti-Marriage Counselor,

If gay and lesbian couples are able to legally marry, it will revolutionize the institution of marriage!

Olivia, Baton Rouge, Louisiana

Dear Olivia,

You may think that David can conquer Goliath, but when you get married, you are turning in your slingshot.

Dear Anti-Marriage Counselor,

We want to get married but be creative and not fall into heterosexual assumptions about our partnership. Any suggestions?

Zelda, Los Angeles

Dear Zelda,

Good Luck. If you absolutely MUST get married, at least be specific about what you can and can't promise. Vows can be challenging, but they ought to reflect reality. For example, any marriage, gay or straight, should probably include the solemn vow, "I promise that if and when we break up I will never speak ill of you to the children."

The most sensible wedding vow I've ever heard was when two lesbian friends of mine looked lovingly at each other during their commitment ceremony, holding hands, and vowed, "I promise to always keep you supplied with chocolate."

It had the ring of truth to it. And at least it's a promise that seems *doable.*

The Gadgetry and the Ecstasy

I've browsed in two of the popular sex shops here in Chicago. I've seen the large selection of "life-size" inflatable dolls. I've seen the shelves stacked with dildos shaped like everything from penises to porpoises to corn-on-the-cob. I've seen the rows of vibrators of all sizes and descriptions. And all the latex vulvas supposedly molded on the real organs of famous porn stars. And the rubber hot water bottle vaginas that supposedly simulate a real warm-body feeling. The handcuffs and the harnesses. And the other paraphernalia from super-clamps to stainless nuts.

The few times I've gone into these sex toy emporiums, I've left feeling not like I've been in a toy store but in a store that sells hospital-patient aids like canes, walkers, and prosthetic devices. To me, an artificial vagina falls into the same category as an artificial hip—not something I'd care to play with.

When lesbian-produced sex videos first became popular, my lover and I rented three of them from one of these shops, to see if they would turn us on. We snuggled up on the sofa to enjoy these latest fruits of lesbian sexual liberation, as they had been championed by *On Our Backs* magazine.

What a disappointment. The first two lesbian sex videos were no more interesting to me than heterosexual porn videos. Which is to say not at all, except maybe as artifacts of some alien culture. They had as much sex appeal as the molded vagina at the sex shop that, according to the blurb on the box, was "So Real You Won't Be Able to Tell the Difference!"

"Maybe we're just not voyeuristic enough to enjoy this kind of thing," I said, as two bland, blemish-free women who might or might not have been lesbians were humping inside our television.

"It's so clinical. Actually it looks kind of ridiculous," said my girlfriend.

The last of the three videos, however, did capture our interest.

In this one, a butchy-looking woman unzips her jeans and pulls a dildo out of her fly. Closeup shot of the dildo: it is a large imitation circumcised penis, just like the kind sold in the sex shops. (If memory serves, this one was purple in color, in keeping with the lesbian theme.) Another woman—femmy-looking—is delighted to see this flexible plastic schlong bobbing out of the butch's pants. She runs over, kneels down, and begins giving a long and enthusiastic blow job to the butch's dildo.

"I thought this was supposed to be *lesbian* porn," I said.

My lover shrugged. "From what we've seen so far, I'd say the industry is still in its infancy."

Then, to our amazement, the woman wearing the dildo began writhing around energetically as if she could actually feel some intense sensations from this inanimate rubbery thing between her legs. As if it were a real penis.

My girlfriend and I sat there totally perplexed.

"What am I missing here?" she said, beginning to laugh.

"How bizarre."

This writhing on the part of the butch went on, gathering momentum, for minutes. She made faces. She grimaced. She moaned.

"Maybe it's like phantom limb syndrome," I said, "where you have referred feeling from something that's been amputated."

"So you think that woman used to be a man?"

"No... I mean, well, I have no idea."

The truth is, I've never understood the appeal of dildos, especially ones that look just like detached penises. What would a lesbian want it for? As a friend of mine says, "Not needing a penis—either to have or to have inserted—is one of the perks of being a lesbian." I feel pretty much the same way. To me a dildo is a kind of boring vestigial appendage. I figured that no lesbians gave much thought to penises, but judging from this video, I was mistaken.

"Maybe it's a social commentary on the state of lesbian politics," my lover mused, smiling mischievously.

"Like what?"

"Oh, that lesbians are still fixated on the symbol of raw male power, pulling and straining against it, only it's just a chunk of plastic?"

"Nice try," I said.

"Or a commentary on American consumerism."

"I do think it's a commentary on American consumerism, but I don't think they intended it to be."

We all know that Americans love gadgets. And we are the world's greatest consumers. We have this naive optimism in America that whatever the problem, we should be able to invent a machine to fix it.

Though I much prefer the feel of living lesbian on my own lesbian skin, my modest little hand-held vibrator has been a Li'l Ms. Fixit now and then during a few stretches between girlfriends. The right tool for the right job. On the other hand, automation in America has taken many people's jobs away. The penetration of sex gadgets into the wider marketplace makes you wonder how long it will be before one's sex life becomes fully automated, too.

Granted, motorized machines are excellent at performing repetitive motions, and can go on performing them as long as the Energizer Bunny can bang that drum. There are no awkward human interactions to worry about. And certain gadgets that aren't even primarily sex toys can be pretty arousing; having a motorcycle between your legs is like a vibrator, only a thousand times more so.

But in this scene in the video, it was the women who were doing all the work, and getting all worked up.

"See—it is symbolic. It's just like corporate capitalism," said my lover. "Women expending all their energy over some dildo who just sits there, the big boss, the center of everybody's attention, even though he's a completely inanimate object. No ideas of his own. No idea of what's going on around him..."

"We might as well have rented *Lethal Weapon*," I said, yawning.

Of course it's to the advantage of sex toy manufacturers to get people to use their products more and more, like the tobacco growers try to get people to smoke. Once we are completely hooked on sexual "accessories" like Pavlovian dogs, our real sex organs will start to salivate at the very sound of the buzzing vibrator, the mere hint of polyvinyl chloride.

Depending on the toy, I don't think using most sex toys is a dangerous habit, the way smoking is. But I'm sure you can get just as addicted. Hooked. Cuffed. Strung out. Some sex toy promoters even disseminate (if I may say so) the suggestion that you can't have good sex at all without their toys and batteries and AC adapters. Next it will be the expensive virtual reality helmets and whatnot. This commercial blitz of fetishism could eventually lead to a new category of sexuality altogether: robosexual: "Who, me? I'm a pomo robo homo."

And when sexual identities get mix-mastered in with our consumer sex gadgetry, will the gadgets become such extensions of ourselves that we feel no civilized person should have to do without them—the way we feel now about our telephones, televisions, and clock-radios? What happens then?

If you can actually imagine some sexual sensation coming from a plastic dildo, it's possible that in the future sex toys could become such sophisticated time- and energy-saving devices, they might even have your entire orgasm for you.

The butch with the purple dildo in the lesbian sex video was well on her way to exactly that. She kept writhing and moaning and puffing, working as hard as a chicken trying to lay a plastic ostrich egg. Every time the femme did some new movement with her mouth, the butch acted as if she felt it right through the polyethylene, or polyurethane, or whatever it was made of.

"The turn-on's got to be mostly visual," I said. "What could be going through her head to act like she could really *feel* that other woman's mouth on a plastic dildo?"

"What's going through her head," said my lover, "is the thought of her paycheck from the video company."

But I wasn't so sure. What if she really was feeling something? People used to mumble about the dangers of sexual objectification, of reducing humans to mere objects of gratification. But I began to wonder if there might be just as much danger in endowing sex toys with a human dimension, elevating inanimate objects to the status of having human feelings—like this woman in the video was doing with the dildo, by giving it nerve endings it couldn't possibly have.

Just a few weeks ago, I saw, in the Winter Catalog of *Lesbian Connection*, an ad selling reasonably priced dildos and dildo harnesses "because you shouldn't have to take out a loan just to have fun sex!"

A loan? Why spend any money on this stuff at all? Even if you can't reach orgasm without the aid of some object, why not personalize the toys by making your own? It would be a lot cheaper cutting out the middleman. Lesbians who are handy at building gadgets could make—and probably have made—some very inventive new toys right in their garage workshops. For example, talking dildos, like talking dolls: you pull on a string, and instead of saying "Math is hard" a recorded voice could say, "That was wonderful, sweetheart. You're the best."

Some lesbian, somewhere, has probably even dated a dildo. Can't you just picture the two of them, sitting across the table from each other in a romantic restaurant with soft music playing? She has such warm, tender feelings toward it for all the pleasure it's given her. The woman and the dildo each have a glass of wine in front of them. It's their sixth anniversary. "Remember, darling," she says, that night we were snowed in together....?" Whoever else may have been there is now lost to her memory—but the dildo has been forever faithful.

The most insidious form of sex gadgetry devised so far—aside from virtual reality, which few people have access to right now—may be phone sex, since the gadget isn't placed in proximity to your crotch but your head, the real center of so much of our sexuality.

And phone sex appears to be a much more lucrative business than the relatively small-ticket items from the sex shops. It looks like a lot of people are hooked on phonics. Months after we saw those insipid lesbian sex videos, my lover and I were watching a late-night movie on television. The commercial time was almost entirely taken up with phone sex ads.

"Someone *sincere*, that's what I want more than anything..." said a pouty blonde with a breathy voice.

She was immediately followed by a pouty brunette. "Just *one special person* to talk to..." The 900 number flashed beneath her.

"Then why don't they just get together with each other?" I said.

"They probably will," said my lover, "after they've clocked in their eight hours of being sincere with that one special phone caller for four bucks a minute."

Wet & Wild

"This will be your first time at the Michigan Festival? Oh, wow, you're going to absolutely love it!" said a friend of mine who had been going to the festival for years. "Even if you don't like to go camping—believe me, you'll love it!"

This was at a party, just five days before I left for the woods with my little tent, my cookstove, my flashlight, my typewriter, my books, my teakettle, my Earl Grey tea bags...

"It's like nothing else you've ever experienced," her friend had agreed, as we'd stood around at the party sipping white wine.

So now I am at the infamous Michigan festival itself, up in the woods, sure enough, here in my little tent. It's ten p.m. and rain is pelting down so hard it sounds like I am going through an automatic car wash. About every fifteen seconds an intense flash lights up the pitch black night and almost instantly ka-POW! Thunder blasts the earth.

"Once you get up there, it's a whole different world," my friend had said.

I am desperately trying to blow up my cheap vinyl air mattress so I can put it under my sleeping bag before the growing puddles and rivulets of water on the tent floor engulf my bedding, my clothes, my books, and my typewriter.

"Imagine all these half-naked lesbians, and lots of women cavorting around with nothing on at all."

"It's a fantastic place to meet women," the other one had said, nudging me with her arm.

Hunched inside my little canvas bubble, I take deep breaths, trying to inflate the air mattress. A good place to meet women? I might as well be in a diving bell at fifty fathoms. I would have had far better luck meeting women if I'd just stayed in Chicago this weekend and gone to a lesbian bar.

"You'll meet so many lesbians you could just cream in your

pants," they both said, giggling.

Indeed, I am totally wet—but not in any way I'd anticipated.

"Anything can happen up there. You'll see."

Every time another blast of lightning hits, the ground trembles. I contemplate my mortality. I can vividly imagine how it would feel if the tall tree right next to my tarp was struck by a bolt and fell directly on my flimsy little tent.

"I know you're shy. But go to the workshops—you'll meet lots of women there."

Next day the rain is falling in sheets. All my clothes that aren't soaked through are damp, but I put on my rain poncho and venture out to the workshops.

The workshops are all held outdoors, of course. We sit in circles on the wet ground, under our ponchos, all of us drenched. We try to ignore the rain, but the sound of it is so loud that we have to shout to hear each other. Water drips from our hair and even from the tips of our noses as we attempt to discuss lesbian culture, lesbian sexuality, lesbian politics. Instead of doing something wet and wild, all of us are simply trying to keep warm and dry.

"You'll see—it's so different, being out there in nature with all those women *au natural!!*" my friend had assured me.

Right now I am also recalling something my mother used to say: "Some people don't have enough sense to come in out of the rain."

Women are leaving the land in droves this afternoon, but several roads are washed out. Cars, vans, trailers are getting stuck in the mud. It is approaching an emergency situation.

"Yeah. The first thing a lot of lesbians do when they find themselves in the woods with other lesbians, and no men around, is to take all their clothes off. Almost like shedding all their inhibitions. It's very tribal," my friend at the party had said.

I told them both I would be far too shy to take off my clothes, unless it was in the privacy of my own tent with somebody I'd invited in to join me.

"You may have no intention of taking your clothes off, but when you get up there, ha ha, it will seem different," they'd said, winking.

As the mud builds up at the festival, many women just give up trying to fight the weather. Dozens of them strip off whatever they have on and belly flop into the huge mud puddles. They attempt gymnastic maneuvers. They slip, slide, and fall over each other like lungfish in primeval ooze. Then, entirely encrusted with mud, they run, laughing, down the road to the showers. I am ready for a shower myself, from all the grit I've accumulated. But the line is long and the shower water is unbelievably cold.

"And be sure to check out the crafts area. The crafts are really fantastic," my friends had said.

I slog through the ubiquitous mud to the crafts area. Here, I happen to run into two lesbians I know at one of the booths. Neither one has a shirt on, and they carry on a conversation with me in the pelting rain just as if the sun was shining, and as if neither of them were naked from the waist up.

"Actually, you get used to seeing women with no clothes on pretty quickly."

Tonight the stars are clear and sparkling above the damp field of thousands of women at the night stage. Then lightning flashes appear on the horizon, and fast-moving storm clouds roll in, till one by one the stars are obscured. It begins to pour again.

"Oh—and wait till you try taking one of those showers! Ha ha! There's no warm water at all. Ha ha!"

I am more wet than ever, and now very grungy too, so I try again to take a shower. It is two o'clock in the morning. At this hour, there are no long lines—just me and one other woman trying clumsily to negotiate the shower spigots by flashlight, crunching our feet awkwardly on the pebbles strewn around the shower area. The freezing water hits me like little spicules of ice.

"Something just comes over you up there," one of my friends at the party had gone on. "You're away from your everyday routine, and you do things that you'd never dream of doing normally."

Lucky for me, it is a very warm night, so at least I will not get pneumonia from my shower. I am about to dry off with my damp towel and put my damp clothes back on when suddenly there is another heavy downpour and everything gets drenched. The rainwater, I notice, is a lot warmer and more pleasant than the shower water.

My jeans are soaking wet, and it seems silly to put them on again. Under the circumstances, there doesn't seem to be any particular point in putting any of my clothes back on. Though it feels kind of weird to me, I begin walking down the country road back to my tent wearing only my soggy sneakers that squish with each step.

The woods are filled with women's tents, pitched much closer to each other than I'd imagined they'd be. Some of the tents are lit up from the inside. All the way down the road, different colored tents glow softly, diffusely—orange, blue, green, red, purple, and khaki domes and triangles.

"Once you get up there, you might do something really wild, something you'd never imagined doing before."

Walking down this country road in the dark woods, soaking wet and stark naked, carrying my wad of wet clothes under one arm, I begin to feel that my friends might have been right—this experience is kind of unique. Kind of freeing. Kind of wild.

This is certainly something I would never consider doing in Chicago. Or anywhere else, except on a private piece of women-only land.

Other women are walking up the road, some with ponchos on, some also naked. The beams of our flashlights cut through the dark, each one a bright cone of light ending a few feet above the ground, leaving everyone looking naked yet somehow strangely disembodied. We greet each other cheerfully as we pass.

I have walked about a mile in my squishing sneakers. It is now close to three a.m. I can hear the distant sounds of drumming. My sneakers squish to the rhythm. The rain has cleared again, and I can see the moon through the clouds. I turn off my flashlight, because it's light enough to dimly see the road without it.

Suddenly seized by some deep but obscure emotion, I start howling up at the moon, loud as I can.

I've never done anything like this before. I do it again.

It feels absolutely marvellous.

Then I come to my senses, and realize I must be waking some campers up. I wait, expecting to hear yelling from the tents, people telling me to shut up, to keep quiet.

Instead, from out of the darkness, a few other women start howling back at me.

Aa-ooooo-oooooo. Yip yip. Aaauuuuuwwwwwwrrrrrhhhh.

I am still very wet, and I feel really good. Naked in the moonlight, I'm discovering for myself the primitive resonating magic of the age-old call of the wild.

WHERE NO
DYKE
HAS GONE
BEFORE

Every time lesbians kiss, another angel gets her wings.

—Roseanne, during a holiday episode of her popular TV comedy show.

Dykosaurus

I saw a copy of the *Weekly World News* in one of the checkout racks of my local supermarket. The cover story was: "Loch Ness Monster is Dead!" A big "photo" of the dying beast showed her massive body beached like a whale, her flippers sadly, helplessly askew.

I had no choice but to buy that paper.

Some people are embarrassed to be seen purchasing the *Weekly World News*, but to me it's like astrology: you don't have to believe what it says to be entertained by it—unless you *want* to. And we all tend to believe what we want to believe.

I've followed the sightings of the elusive Loch Ness Monster "Nessie" in the *Weekly World News* for some years now, along with the more frequent Elvis sightings. I've also felt compelled to purchase the issues with front page pictures of politicians chatting with an alien (the outer space, not the illegal, kind) about the state of the world.

I don't think the *Weekly World News* fabricates *all* their bizarre stories—after all, we do live in a world where someone actually had the wrong foot amputated, and I don't doubt that somebody somewhere left $14 million to their poodle.

So what's so implausible about the existence of a giant prehistoric aquatic beast who survived the extinction of all the rest of the dinosaurs sixty-five million years ago, only to become trapped in an isolated Scottish lake after the last Ice Age receded, and paddled about underwater all the way down to modern times?

An awful lot of people claim to have seen her. And I say "her" because I've no doubt that Nessie is female. The *Weekly World News* concurs in this opinion. But—and here's something the tabloids haven't figured out yet—I feel certain that the Loch Ness Monster is also a lesbian.

Of course she's cautious and stays out of sight! Of course she's "elusive"! She's resigned to never entirely coming out, and feels that for safety's sake she must hide forever in the murky mists of Loch Ness—the world's deepest freshwater closet.

How do I know that Nessie is a friend of Dorothy? First of all, because of the type of dinosaur she is. Second, because she's survived against such impossible odds. Third, because so many people doubt that she exists despite frequent sightings.

Many scientists have noted that the mysterious Nessie, with her long, supple neck, barrel-like body, and flippers, closely resembles a type of extinct marine dinosaurs which lived throughout the waters of the Eastern Hemisphere from the Late Triassic through the Late Jurassic epochs (230 to 144 million years ago). Some forms of this dinosaur group are known to have lived until the very end of the dinosaur era, at the end of the Cretaceous Period, 66.4 million years ago. Those who believe that Nessie is a dinosaur agree that she is a direct genetic link to this extinct group.

The name of this dinosaur group is the plesiosaurs.

Plesiosaur (pronounced p-lezzie-o-sor). This disguised lesbian reference suggests that the first scientists to study Nessie's link with these aquatic dinosaurs knew full well that she was a lesbian creature. The initial p was their attempt to muffle the real meaning of the technical name, since plain old "lesiosaur" would have made it too obvious. Those learned 19th century fossil-hunters probably intended the 'p' to be silent, as in so many Greek-derived words, so the hidden meaning would still be clear to scholars and other well-educated homosexuals.

The plesiosaur was a versatile beast. She could use her paddle-like limbs to swim backwards as well as forwards, and even to rotate herself around her body axis. Just like Nessie. Early plesiosaurs were relatively small, about 15 feet long, but as time went on they grew to be as large as 43 feet long. Their snakelike necks and heads alone accounted for half their length.

Nessie has continued to grow over time, and is estimated to be a whopping sixty-two feet today—a real big-boned gal.

Was she always a lesbian? I believe so. We can imagine Nessie as a young lesiosaur in a kind of pristine Lesbian dinosaur Eden. Frolicking among the early segmented marine arthropodyka with her other dykosaur friends in long ago, far happier times. She probably fell in love with some other bright-eyed eager-to-pleasiosaur, and they winked flirtatiously at each other with their nictitating membranes as the pterodyktyls flew far above, and the Sapphosauruses and the Diplodykuses munched tender ginkgo leaves at the water's edge.

Before the meteors came. Before the deadly cloud of dust. Long before the ice.

And then, tragic Nessie! For centuries she swam around the northern reaches of Inverness, brokenhearted, as the ice melted into the highland crags. So lonely! She became a legend, the subject of ancient prophecies. And in modern times, the target of tourists, of fanatic people shlepping scuba equipment around castle ruins, and of scientists piloting submarines through the Loch to try to flush her out and thereby get their grants renewed.

But no one could fathom her.

Then the *Weekly World News* reported that Nessie had been captured in December of 1991 with an enormous steel net—and she was pregnant! A few months later came an encouraging update: because of the "world outcry," her scientist-captors had released Nessie, and hours later—on March 21, 1992—she gave birth to a wee *baby* Loch Ness Monster. There were photos, too, of Nessie and baby swimming together, and of a diver patting Nessie's head underwater.

Well, no wonder she's so protective of her privacy—she's not only a lesbian, but a lesbian mom!

They called the baby Dino-Mite. Naturally I called her Dyko-Mite. Another female, of course, since she would have to have been produced by parthenogenesis.

The *Weekly World News* didn't even wonder where this single mom's baby came from. Idiots! But of course they wouldn't know about lesbian parthenogenesis.

Naturally when I saw this newest alarming headline, "Loch Ness Monster Dies!," I was concerned not only about Nessie but also about who was going to take proper care of three-year-old Dyko-Mite if her mom was gone.

Then I took a closer look at the *Weekly World News* cover picture of the dying Loch Ness Monster. It shows a crowd of gapers at the water's edge staring at her in her plight after this shy creature had supposedly "beached herself." These people are oddly dressed in 1950s style polo-shirts and bathing suits, and sporting outmoded haircuts.

Scotland can't be *that* far behind the times.

Which means this photo is a fake!

The *Weekly World News* isn't exactly risking their journalistic reputation by fabricating a story. But what would motivate them to perpetrate such a hoax? Aside from boosting their circulation, I mean.

Then suddenly I understood. The tabloids *know!* I thought they hadn't figured it out, but they *did!* They put two tons and two tons together and realized that Nessie is a lezzie, a camp girl, a member of the lodge, a green lima bean, auch eye, a hundred points!

That's why they'd never speculated at all as to who the baby's father was!

Discovering that one of their star headliners was a very much alive "extinct" dykosaur was just too much for them. So they did something unconscionable, those homophobic pricks! They decided to do away with her! They concocted this flashy cover story about her untimely death!

Nessie's snaky face looks very cute in the phony photo, I must say. But they've positioned her sinewy neck so that it seems to be broken, twisted at a sharp, "unnatural" angle. Here they made another slip in their story, by graphically revealing that they think she's into something "unnatural."

Since the story of Nessie's death is clearly a hoax, this can only mean one thing: she's eluded them again.

She's still alive!

It's up to us—lesbian and gay activists and animal lovers and queer paleontologists—to encourage Nessie not to give up the fight for survival when she's come so very far, and to keep working toward a world in which it will be truly safe for a genuine prehistoric lesiosaur family to come out of hiding at long last.

If the Shoe Fits

There are over seven hundred versions of the story of Cinderella. I've read that it's the most well-known fairy tale of all time.

Now, I've been accused of seeing lesbians in places where there aren't any. From my perspective, I think I simply find lesbians in places that other people never thought to look.

I saw the Disney version of *Cinderella* when I was a child, and never thought about the possibility that Cinderella might be a lesbian. But not long ago it occurred to me that if there are seven hundred versions of Cinderella, at least a few of those versions *must* have some as-yet undetected lesbian content.

Or maybe Cinderella herself is a metaphor for the lesbian social condition? After all, lesbians are kept locked in the attic of society while their straight sisters are busy trying to impress some Prince Charming or other. Unappreciated, unthanked, taken for granted, asked to tiptoe around and yet be there when straight friends need a shoulder to cry on, and even clean up their romantic messes. Lesbians have been left to sweep the dirty hearths of heterosexuals for hundreds of years now.

So was Cinderella some kind of a broom-closet lesbian?

I traced the historical accounts of Cinderella to see. I couldn't find any obvious queer symbolism. But I discovered that the Disney film with the singing mice is a prettied-up version of a much more gruesome story.

The origin of the Cinderella tale appears to be China, where the earliest known version was written down around 850 A.D. The basic theme is the importance of having very tiny feet—in other words, it's a promotional vehicle for the practice of footbinding.

In this very first version, the major elements of the story are already present. A mean stepmother mistreats her stepdaughter Yeh-hsien, and forces her to wear rags. Yeh-hsien wishes upon the bones of a magic fish and she's granted a beautiful outfit so she can go to a festival, where she leaves behind a golden slipper. A rich merchant comes into possession of the slipper, and he searches everywhere for the woman who can fit into such a tiny shoe. At the end of the story, the stepmother and her bigfooted—therefore ugly—daughter are buried under a hail of stones.

From China, the story moved round the world, with different names and details, but the original idea persists: the woman with the smallest feet wins love from the most wealthy, eligible man. In an old Scottish version the lone stepdaughter became three stepsisters, the wish was granted by a magic calf rather than a fish, the slipper was satin, and the rich merchant was elevated to the status of a Prince. Perhaps in keeping with the starkness of Celtic traditions, this stepmother actually cuts off the toes and heel of her eldest daughter to get the shoe to fit. In some versions the Prince detects the ruse because he sees blood leaking from the slipper.

Disney based his 1949 animated film on a French version published in 1697 by Charles Perrault. Perrault's version was tamer, and included the fairy godmother and a royal ball. His heroine has to sweep cinders from the hearth—the dirtiest job in the house—hence the name Cinderella. His version was also the first in which the slipper was made of glass. Disney's *Cinderella* came on the heels, so to speak, of his huge success with *Snow White*. The protective dwarfs have been transformed into singing mice (mice always being a sure bet for Disney) who are threatened by an evil cat just as Cinderella is threatened by her stepmother.

I remembered that Disney's Cinderella talked to animals, but that didn't necessarily make her a lesbian. Still, I just couldn't get it out of my mind that there was something pink-triangular going on in the story. So I got a video of the Disney cartoon. I hadn't seen it in years. Now everything has fallen into place. It's a gay tale beyond any doubt—but not the way I thought. I discovered an entire level of characterization that had never quite made sense until now.

Disney's Cinderella is as saccharin sweet as I remembered her. She is lovely, delightful, sings beautifully, is hardworking and courteous and skilled at all the traditional women's tasks like sewing—a genuinely nice person who puts up with a level of shit from her stepsisters and her cruel stepmother that just about anyone else would find intolerable.

But she also appears to be kind of stupid, completely pliable, and relatively spiritless. She rarely questions authority. She has very strict gender notions and has educated all the mice in proper sex roles. In her limited spare time she makes dresses and bonnets for the female mice, and jackets and shoes and little pointed hats (but no pants!) for the male mice. When she hears that a new mouse is stuck in the trap, her first thought is modesty—not to run and save this mouse but to clothe it. She picks out a dress for little Gus, but the other mice tell her it's a boy. "Oh," she says, "that *does* make a difference," and takes out a tiny shirt.

I'm sorry, but this is not your typical dyke profile at all.

And by the way, Disney's animators solved the problem of making her feet look tiny by eliminating toes altogether. Whenever her feet are bare, she simply *has* no toes. Cinderella is so graceful and swanlike that she doesn't need them in order to walk.

The key to the whole queer underpinning of Disney's story is not Cinderella but the King, who has an extraordinarily high level of anxiety, adamantly insisting that the Prince be married as soon as possible.

"My son has been avoiding his responsibilities long enough!" blusters the King. "It's high time he married and settled down."

The Grand Duke tells the King he must be patient. The King will not hear of it. The Prince has been away and is about to come home, so the King plans a ball for that very night. The King says, "If all the eligible maidens just happen to be there—why, he's bound to show interest in one of them, isn't he? ISN'T HE?" He screams and collars the Grand Duke. "It can't possibly fail, can it?"

This King is portrayed as a desperate man. He's afraid he won't ever have grandchildren. Why? Because the Prince has no interest in women. This point is stressed over and over in the movie. It's hard to avoid the conclusion that the reason the King is so anxious is that he's afraid his son is a homosexual.

I've always found Prince Charming impossibly bland and boring. Not because I'm a lesbian, either. The handsome Prince seems to have no personality at all. I realize now that he isn't boring—he's simply not *there* emotionally. He's hiding all his true feelings. He's been forced to come back to the palace and try to act straight when he'd rather be off with his cruising buddies.

If anything goes wrong with the plan to get the Prince interested in some woman, ANY woman, the King says he will take off the Grand Duke's head. Is the Grand Duke responsible in some way for the Prince's lack of interest in women? My guess is that the King suspects some hanky panky went on between the Prince and the Grand Duke, and that's why the Prince was sent away in the first place.

At the ball, the King watches how perfunctorily his son greets each of the women he's introduced to. "The boy isn't cooperating," he murmurs as the Prince stiffly bows to each maiden.

"I tried to warn you," says the Grand Duke. Maybe the Grand Duke *has* had some hanky panky with the Prince.

Meanwhile, out in the woods, Cinderella's tears have summoned her so-called fairy godmother.

If the fairy godmother really has Cinderella's interests at heart, how come she hasn't shown up a lot earlier, to prevent all the grueling years of housework that Cinderella has already endured being bossed around by her stepmother? I even wondered about that when I was a kid. Why didn't the fairy godmother simply turn the *evil stepmother* into a pumpkin? The answer is: it's because she's really working on behalf of the Prince, not Cinderella. This fairy godmother knows exactly what will attract the attention of a fairy, and it's that impossibly dainty coach with all the froofy grillwork.

"Dance and be gay," says the fairy godmother cryptically, waving Cinderella off to the ball in high drag. Poor unsuspecting Cinderella falls right into the plan. She arrives dressed all in glitter and sparkling, in an ostentatious display of wealth, in her coach with four white horses, driver and footman. Prince Charming is captivated by the image of this glittering vision not because he wants to marry her, but because he wants to BE her.

As a matter of fact, Cinderella's famous glass slippers aren't slippers at all but pumps. And if Cinderella doesn't know the difference, you can be sure the Prince does.

Well, you know what happens next. The clock strikes twelve. The King is dreaming of royal grandchildren when the Grand Duke comes in to break the news that the mysterious babe in the bell-shaped dress has vanished.

"You were in league with the Prince all along!" the King screams. "The whole thing was a plot!"

What kind of a plot might that be? This elaborate ball that has flushed out every virgin in the surrounding countryside is designed just for the Prince to find any woman he likes, and the only one he claimed to like no longer exists. Who does the King think she was? Harvey Fierstein in a Dolly Parton wig?

If you go back and read the Perrault version of the story, this is what it says: "It happened that the King's son gave a ball and invited all persons of fashion to it." The Prince had no problem finding a woman he liked in the version Disney used as his source. There were eight story writers on the Disney project—all men. One or more of them had to have deliberately infused the animated storyline with homosexual content!

The explicit fear of male homoeroticism is even shown on screen. After the spell has worn off, Cinderella, back in her old ragged clothes again, tells the mice how wonderful and romantic an evening it was. Gus dreamily snuggles up to his mouse friend Jacques, who rather absentmindedly puts his arm around Gus. When Jacques realizes that he's in a romantic posture with another male mouse, he jumps back and gives Gus a pointedly suspicious look. This is not a gesture meant for the kiddies.

Now here's what clinches the whole thing for me. After the ball, knowing the pressure that's on him to get married, and perhaps fearful of exposure, the Prince reverses himself and decides to play to form. He agrees to marry *any woman whose foot fits into the glass slipper!* Either he's as stupid as Cinderella, or he's figured out that sooner or later he's going to have to marry somebody or people will be talking.

So—is Cinderella a lesbian? No. But Prince Charming is definitely a bigtime closet case torn between his sense of duty as future king and his gay lifestyle. He has to keep up appearances and every hint of propriety. He sees in Cinderella someone so pliable and sexually naive that she will never even suspect him. And he's right—Cinderella's no modern Princess Di or trendy Duchess of York—she's never even heard the phrase "fag hag."

How long can such a marriage last? I guess it could actually go on forever after—because Prince Charming is such a great improvement over Cinderella's previous situation in the scullery that she's dazed with her good luck! What a setup for him! When her husband stays away all night, she'll only blame herself for not being woman enough to keep her man from seeking comfort in another woman's arms!

Here's the tragic postscript to the story of this poor straight woman landing her Prince Charming:

Too ashamed to tell her troubles to anyone (and with no lesbian friends' shoulders to cry on) but determined to make good use of her time, Cinderella will diligently—almost obsessively—keep sewing more little shirts for Gus and Jacques—and the female birds can always use some new babushkas.

It will never cross her mind to complain about Prince Charming's evenings at the male-only club, his long absences to go gambling and carousing with the boys. And she will never ever imagine the true reason for all those visits to confer with dukes, knights, squires, coachmen, footmen…

She will think it must be out of pity for her loneliness that her lovely ladies-in-waiting keep giving her fond looks and inviting her up to their parlors in the palace for a nightcap.

Northern Exposure

"Christmas is in the air!" says the ad for holiday music CDs. My calendar says it's mid-October, not even Halloween yet, but 'tis the season my mailbox becomes inundated with catalogs of Christmas items so the annual frenzied consumerism can begin. To get in the holiday mood, I can order albums that will surround me with the sounds of a Celtic Christmas, an Irish Christmas, a Polish Christmas, a German Christmas, a monk-chanting medieval Gregorian Christmas, and a Kwanzaa song medley. I can alternate Handel's *Messiah* with a nostalgic carolling barbershop quartet. I can even listen to Mannheim Steamroller "give a New Age twist to holiday classics."

But one Christmas album I want to hear is absent from these catalog offerings. I mean the Venus Envy recording *I'll be a Homo for Christmas*, including such wonderful songs as "Lesbians We Have Heard on High," "Oh Little Town in Michigan," "Rhonda the Lesbo Reindeer," "The Twelve Gays of Christmas *("On the eighth day of Christmas my true love gave to me: eight menstrual sponges, seven vibrators, six pierced labia, five dental dams...!")* and my favorite, the "Chipmunk Commitment" song, in which the lesbian chipmunks sing, *"...Want to start a family, who'll get pregnant, you or me? We can't wait to ovulate, please Christmas don't be late!"*

The closer it gets to Christmas day, the more the din of popular Christmas music I don't want to hear becomes inescapable, and the image of Santa Claus appears everywhere. By the time I was seven-years-old in the mid-1950s, I had started paying particular attention to the lyrics of holiday pop songs. The words of one song I heard impressed themselves on me:

"He sees you when you're sleeping, he knows when you're awake, he knows if you've been bad or good, so be good for goodness sake! Oh—you'd

better watch out, you'd better not cry, you'd better not pout, I'm telling you why: Santa Claus is coming to town."

My neighborhood was not like the Kodak holiday commercials on TV. Santa came in through the fire escape, not the chimney. What was a chimney? I hung my red felt stocking on a clothesline my mother strung up across the hall doorway. And since planes went overhead quite frequently on their way to La Guardia airport, there were a lot of local sleigh-sightings above the el tracks on Christmas eve. Despite these differences from the storybooks, we kids believed that Santa was still Santa, a magic old man who was benevolent and kind to children.

Yet I brooded on the lyrics of that popular holiday song. The portrayal of Santa as a kind of Big Brother of the Yuletide struck me as very sinister. It still does. "You'd better watch out" conveyed something very disturbing. If you were bad, Santa left coal in your stocking. This led me to ask myself: What if, even though I thought I'd been good and done everything right and hadn't told a lie or anything, what if my stocking is filled with coal on Christmas morning?

Of course, at the time I didn't comprehend that the whole modern-day Santa setup was an elaborate lie that adults perpetrate on children. Just like the lie that as gay people, there is something amorphously wrong with us—and we'd better watch out, better not cry, don't ask, don't tell.

This kind of thinking is, as we ex-hippies used to say, a mindfuck. What I find interesting about it now is how closely it can parallel the internal coming out process. It encapsulates the mentality of self-censorship, paranoia, and simplistic thinking that groups like the religious right are trying to foist on us all. No young person today, coming out to themselves, should have to put any energy into struggling to reject the idea that they are flawed or less than good because they find themselves attracted to someone of their own, rather than the "opposite," gender. It's the Christmas Ging-Grinches at work, trying to undermine a person's own perceptions and feelings about what is 'good' and 'bad' and 'normal' and rewarding. Mainstream religion is, for the most part, still telling all of us queers that we deserve to get coal in our stockings. Despite the fact that we've been good, and honest, and truthful, and (unlike some rightwing evangelists) we haven't lied about who we are.

A friend of mine showed me a little illustration from a modern children's book. It shows Santa, in a fur jacket, standing in a circular tower observatory, with icicles hanging down from the windows. He and his dog (German shepherd, of course) both look out at the snow-covered landscape—but Santa is looking through a long old-fashioned spyglass. The caption reads, "Kris Kringle observing an especially nice child."

Still spying after all these years. *He's making a list, checking it twice, gonna find out who's naughty and nice…*

Apparently today's Santa is an amalgam of the fourth century Christian Saint Nicholas who had a reputation for generosity, Norse mythology and Nordic folktales, and the legend of Sinterklaas that Dutch colonists brought to New Amsterdam in the 17th century. American commercial ingenuity added the tie-in with the gifts of the Magi, so that everyone felt obliged to go on a buying spree to give children toys in the guise of an imaginary fairy. And then came Rudolph. And the elves. And Mrs. Claus. And plastic snow. And the Chipmunks.

Every year TV specials muck around with the Santa legend in one way or another. But there's no reason we should let Santa Claus be branded a voyeur and an oppressive agent in the surveillance of children! Such a freespirited fairy elf would never want us to feel bad about ourselves.

And why is Santa, whom everybody concedes is a fairy, always shown as heterosexually married to a housefrau who bakes all the holiday pies and nags him about his drinking?

I know I'm skating on thin ice just bringing up the subject of Santa and sexuality in the same breath. Considering that Santa's such an icon for children, I guess he's not supposed to have any sex life at all. Though it's hardly a stretch to imagine Santa as a dedicated radical fairy. After the holiday work is done, all the fairies and elves throw fabulous fetes with an endless buffet, lots of iced drinks and hot rum punch—one long holiday celebration sponsored by the North Pole chapter of Girth and Mirth.

Myself, I can envision a matriarchal, not a patriarchal, Santa. This Santa's not male at all. She never was. She has that deep commitment to caring and nurturing—well-known female traits. She has the female primal power to soothe the heart of the beast, so reindeer are willing to travel such a hectic frequent flyer schedule with her. And as a lesbian, she knows better than anyone else how to fly the whole world in one night, since dykes are accustomed to festivals that come and go in the twinkling of an eye. She's even got a female first name, ending in an 'a'. If Santa is a "he," how come he's not called Santo Claus, like Santo Domingo?

So, if there is a Santa Claus, she is a mature grandmotherly woman, and furthermore she has been married to her lover, Kristine Kringle, for many years. It's legal up there near the pole, you see. "Mr. and Mrs." Claus-Kringle are very closeted; they have to be, since despite the fact that they are both grannies and the sweetest people you'll ever meet, most parents wouldn't let them near children if they knew they had a satisfying lesbian relationship. Go figure.

I imagine they are a very tight couple, very traditional. The reason their names often get confused is that Kris Kringle and Santa Claus share the responsibility of delivering gifts to the children. They spend the year up there in the frozen tundra where the real estate is cheap and nobody harasses them, Dyking the Halls with the other L'ves in their Northern Lights lesbian commune. Here they can openly practice their L'fin magic and merrily make all sorts of toys. When the holiday rolls around, Santa and Kris don their fluffy red outfits, buckled boots and caps, add some white hair extenders to their beards to fill them out, and no one is the wiser.

It's a Wonderful Life! And not to worry—this Santa doesn't see you when you're sleeping or know when you're awake. She's not interested in prying into what you do under the flannel blankie, alone in your little bed. She believes in privacy *and* free speech, love and good cheer.

When the weather is sunny and the snow has thawed on the pines, Santa gets out her vintage Harley, and she and Kris go with other members of the L'f-and-Fairy motorcycle club on a Toys for Tots campaign. If the weather holds, they may make it as far south as Cicely, Alaska—that enchanted frontier town founded by two lesbians—gathering still more toys for needy children.

The L'ves are happy and eager and full of new ideas for toys. The adult toy division and the children's toy division are not in competition with each other, so nobody has to get uptight. And Santa does not run a sweatshop. She is never grumpy. All the L'ves work together for a common good, bringing hope and comfort to all who believe in them.

Christmas day, back in the icy reaches of the snow-covered North after a delivery job well done, "Mr. and Mrs." Claus-Kringle snuggle warmly under the beautiful antique handmade down quilt made especially for them by their sister L'ves hundreds of years ago. It looks as bright today as the day it was given to them. Downstairs, the other L'ves are mingling, merrily singing, "I'm Dreaming of a Naiad Christmas." Santa and Kris begin to feel those old passions rising, as the snowflakes dance outside their window and the reindeer snort in the haybarn. "Oh, Santa!" Kris murmurs, her breath quickening…

Merry Solstice! Bon Hiver! And may your Yuletide be gay! Living, as we still do, in a society that would keep us isolated and fearful, whenever we come out to each other we are bringing tidings of comfort and joy.

And Yes, Virginia, Santa Claus is a lesbian! She wishes children all round the world peace and happiness and to grow up healthy and full of wonder at this adventure called life—whoever you become and whoever you will love. You can wave to Santa as the reindeer carry her up and away safely back home, sleighbells a-jingling, and you'll hear her laughing a jolly "Ho-ho-ho!

Stake Out

All heads turn as she enters the smoky lesbian bar in an outfit so black that you can't even tell if it's leather or velvet. Her eyes seem to look through you, to hypnotize you. She's a night-person, a little bit batty perhaps—but more seductive than any woman you've ever met before.

It's Dykula, and she wants to invite you home, take off your clothes, make love to you—and then, while you burn in the heat of sexual arousal, what will she do? She will open her mouth very wide, and chomp right through your throbbing neck with her fangs, so she can suck your blood out of your jugular vein. Till you die.

Afterwards she'll dump your body somewhere without another thought, climb into a coffin filled with clumps of dirt and, yawning leisurely, shut the lid.

But hey, that's her thing—so like who am I to criticize, right?

I just don't get it. Is this really anybody's idea of a hot date?

Why, oh, why is everyone except me so fascinated by lesbian vampyres?

When it comes to blood, my motto is: Neither a sucker nor a suckee be. Blood-sucking is not safe, it's not sanitary, and it's certainly not sporting.

And goddess knows it's not pretty to watch. Writers like Anne Rice and Jewelle Gomez can make it sound fascinating on paper, but did you see the scenes in the film version of *Interview with the Vampire* when they have blood-drinking orgies? I mean, was that gross or what?

I don't even like a rare steak.

Of course there is a certain seductive appeal to living forever, youthful looking and invulnerable to the aging process. Seeing the decades and centuries go by, and how life changes.

And the hypnotic powers one has over ordinary mortals—

powers those mortals can barely conceive of.

And flying around on shiny black leathery wings must be a kick.

And I can see why lesbians and gay men might identify with the mythology, too:

Here's a creature who stays out of the daylight but comes alive at dusk. A creature who is part of a secret society of similar creatures. A creature seemingly so rare and elusive that almost nobody believes in its existence. A creature who cruises in the midst of people, unbeknownst to them. A creature people consider a monster when they do realize it exists. A creature people will do anything to keep their loved ones away from.

But then, most of the above applies to serial killers too—which vampyres are, come to think of it.

I grant you that sometimes maybe ingesting just a little bit of blood in the fullness of passion is impossible to avoid. Once after making love I went to the bathroom and glanced in the mirror, and there was blood on my hands and blood all over my face and chest.

Oh my god! I ran back to make sure my partner was all right, and she turned on the light and looked at the bed sheet, and looked at me—and what must have been my mortified expression of concern. And she laughed. "I was three days overdue—and I guess you just brought it on! Thanks! Can I take your picture like that?"

I did not find it funny. Or sexy either. But this was way back before AIDS and safe sex—or my horror might have been more than momentary.

So is this Dykula craze some kind of a menstruation fantasy thing? Or a piercing thing? I really can't figure it out.

An ex-lover of mine was so fascinated by vampires, in fact, that she had a set of upper teeth made for herself with elongated vampire fang canines. She had it crafted by a dental technician, so it slipped on perfectly right over her real teeth.

It wasn't so easy for her to talk with this contraption on, because of course the vampire teeth bumped against her lower lip. But when I saw them on her, that was it. The real source of my vampire aversion dawned on me—no pun intended.

The bottom line is this: I do not want anyone—and I mean *anyone*—going down on me who has fangs.

Hazel and Gretel

Once upon a time, there was a woman named Hazel, who lived all alone in a tiny cottage deep in the heart of a dense forest. Hazel cultivated a small garden, and she kept bees, a few chickens, and a goat. She gathered wood to warm herself in winter. When times were very hard, she managed to survive by digging for turnips, onions, and ginger root and by picking the berries that grew wild in the forest. Hazel did a lot of reading in dusty old books, by the dim yellow light of her oil lamp, and she studied the medicinal properties of many different teas and herbs and insects.

There was a little village on the edge of the forest. People in this village told their children that a powerful, cruel witch named Hazel lived in the heart of the woods, and this horrible old witch liked nothing better than to trap tasty little children and eat them up. They only said this because they wanted their children to stay out of the deep forest, where they were liable to get lost. Perhaps a few of these people also enjoyed frightening children. But after awhile, some of the villagers began to believe their own stories.

A woodcutter and his wife lived in this village. They had a son named Hans. One day the woodcutter, who was often very drunk, came after the boy with an ax, and Hans ran deep into the forest to get away from his father. After dark, Hans became lost and afraid. He tripped over a tree-stump, bumping his head, and scraping his knees and his chin. He sat down, bleeding, and cried pitifully.

After awhile, he saw a small light approaching. It was Hazel, with her oil lamp. She had heard his cries. Hazel brought the boy back to her humble cottage. She applied soothing poultices to his knees and chin and the bump on his head. She let the injured boy sleep in her own little bed, while she slept on a mat on the floor near the hearth. In the morning Hans was hungry. Hazel baked some fresh gingerbread from the meager stores of flour she kept in a jar for special occasions. Hans had never had gingerbread before. They had a lovely talk for several hours. Then Hazel showed Hans the path back out of the forest.

But Hans didn't want to leave the nice lady. His mother and father were never so kind to him. Hazel allowed the boy to stay two more days while his knees healed up. They made up songs together and played games. He helped Hazel with her little garden. She let him feed the hardened breadcrumbs to the chickens. But then, thinking that his parents would be frantic, and that it was high time he should be back in school, Hazel convinced Hans he must go. Hans was a thoughtful, considerate child, and he realized that the nice lady had but little for herself, much less for two, so he resigned himself to going home, promising to come back to visit.

When Hans got back, his parents were no longer angry, but worried and embarrassed. They didn't want their neighbors to know that the boy had run off into the woods to get away from them. When they found out where Hans had been, they told all the other townspeople that the witch of the woods had lured the child into her house, and locked him up, and that he had barely escaped with his life.

"That Old Witch Hazel…she's got a big mansion out there in the woods, made of, uh, what's it made of, boy?"

Hans knew that his parents would beat him if he didn't support their story. He didn't know what to say. He blurted out the first thing he could think of. "Gingerbread," he said, hanging his head. "And candy and cake."

"You hear that?! She was trying to fatten the child up to eat him! Isn't that right, Hans? She wanted to cook him for dinner! She's a cannibal, that ugly old witch! Why, there must be bones of other poor children buried all over the place out there…"

"What were you doing so deep in the forest, boy?" someone asked.

He looked at his parents, who looked back at him sternly. "I was playing in the woods and I got lost." He began to cry. "I tried to find my way home with some breadcrumbs I had in my pocket," he babbled, "but birds ate them…"

Many of the townspeople muttered among themselves that it was time to do something about that crazy old witch who was a menace to their village.

Now, Hans's teacher at school was a spinster named Gretel. She was worried about the boy. She saw the bruises he came to school with, and knew he wasn't getting into fights with other boys. And she saw how withdrawn he had become. She thought his story sounded very mixed-up—but if it was even partially true, all the children were in danger.

So Gretel ventured into the forest to see this Old Witch Hazel herself. After several hours of walking in the dense wood, she came to the witch's little run-down cottage. She knocked on the door, her heart pounding with fear, expecting to be confronted with a mean, ugly old witch with burning red eyes. When Hazel opened the door, Gretel found herself gazing into the kindest, loveliest eyes she had ever seen.

Hazel was delighted to have another visitor. She invited Gretel in and made her a cup of camomile tea. Hazel was astonished to hear the story Hans had been telling in town. She couldn't believe the boy would say such awful things. "My goodness, if I had a whole house made out of gingerbread, and cake, and candy, why would I want to cook and eat tough little children?" she said, laughing.

Gretel was impressed with Hazel's logical mind, and the way her eyes crinkled up when she laughed.

"In the first place, I'm a vegetarian. The forest creatures are my friends. "

Gretel was impressed with Hazel's kindness to animals. But she saw that Hazel did not appreciate the seriousness of her situation. "The townspeople have always said that you were a witch."

"A witch?" said Hazel with alarm. "What does that mean? I only know a lot about herbs and potions and how to heal certain injuries."

Gretel was impressed by Hazel's sincerity and unassuming nature. "But why do you live way out here in the woods?" she asked.

"I grew up here. After my parents died, I stayed on. It's my home." She smiled at Gretel.

"But don't you get lonely out here all by yourself?"

"Sometimes," Hazel said sadly. She sighed heavily.

Gretel was impressed by Hazel's bosom as it rose and fell.

During the next month, every day she had off from teaching, Gretel was drawn to visit the woman in the woods. On one of these visits, Gretel felt bold enough to give Hazel a kiss. It was the beginning of the spring. Buds were blooming. Gretel's heart began to sing. The world had become a wonderful enchanted place. After that, Gretel found herself spending all her free time at the sweet little cottage with Hazel.

Then one day Hans came to school with a black eye, and when Gretel took him aside, he cried and confessed that he had made up the story about the wicked witch—that it was his parents' doing. And now they had begun hurting him again.

Gretel went to Hans's house to talk with his parents. They were both drunk. When they found out why she had come, they told her to stay out of their business.

"You've been going into the woods a lot lately yourself, haven't you, teacher?" said Hans's father menacingly, as he staggered around the kitchen.

"Yes, she has," said Hans's mother, steadying herself against the table. "That Old Witch has bewitched you, too! You're helping her trap our children, now, aren't you?!"

"Oh, you hateful creatures!" said Gretel. She turned to leave. "Hans? Where are you, dear?"

Hans's mother leaped at Gretel and attacked her with a poker. Gretel pushed her away, and the woman slipped and fell with a great clatter, and practically tumbled into the open door of the oven.

Gretel ran out. Knowing the superstitions of the townsfolk, she realized what was liable to happen. She gathered up her clothes and a few possessions, and ran back into the woods.

When the angry villagers arrived at Hazel's house that night, their torches burning, they found no one at home. They were disappointed to see that the humble cottage was not made of gingerbread and cake. "She's lifted the spell out of spite, damn her," said one villager, "so we can't even make off with her gingerbread."

"She's a witch all right," said another, emerging from the cottage. "Here's the proof!" He held Hazel's broom up for everyone to see, and they got so mad that they torched the little cottage and burned it to the ground. They vowed that if they ever saw that witch again, they'd do the same to her.

But they never did see her again.

Hans, tortured by guilt, hid under his parents' house all that night. He ran away from home for the last time when he was fourteen, and his parents never heard from him again. They swore that their son's life had been ruined by that wicked old witch.

As the years passed, the story became more and more jumbled through many retellings at the village tavern. In their drunkenness, Hans's name got slurred with Hazel's into "Hanzel," while the name of the witch was forgotten. What difference did it make to them? She was the Wicked Witch, and that was name enough. Gretel became another captive of the witch's spell, who shoved her into the oven. At long last, the parents themselves even got Gretel mixed up with Hans, and thought they remembered two children who had been lost in the woods.

The sensational story of a wicked old witch was a lot more interesting to tell than the all-too-common story of violent parents who beat and threaten their own children. So the witch-tale was the version that got passed down through time, frightening many more generations of children.

Our story, too is almost done, but our ending is happy and not at all Grimm. Hazel and Gretel moved to a wonderful land over the mountains, where they could live together openly as lesbians and everyone thought it was a fine thing that they were so happy together. Hazel became famous as a local healer, and Gretel was able to teach school again.

One day, ten years later, Hans, in his long vagrant wanderings, happened to show up in their town, and they had a lovely reunion. Hazel told Hans she had never blamed him for lying about her—that she knew it hadn't been his fault. They found him a job, and he settled nearby, and visited often. He always treated the two women respectfully, and loved them as if they were his real parents, as he wished they had been.

And they all lived happily ever after.

The Lowlander

She was born four hundred years ago in the Lowlands of Holland. Her name is Dyckan MacProud, and she is Immortal…

Dyckan MacProud cannot die, unless another Immortal cuts off her head. She lives on a houseboat in Paris where she sells antiques, or in some American city where she runs a martial arts center, depending on the season and the viewer demographics.

There are many Immortals, more and more in every episode. Some are good and some are bad, but every single one of them is queer! Isn't that amazing? In four hundred years, Dyckan MacProud of the van-MacProuds has never once, so far as we know, encountered an openly heterosexual Immortal of either gender!

None of the other Immortals, some of whom are a lot older than Dyckan, ever met a straight person either, anywhere in the world on their centuries-long travels! That kind of glaring omission might leave some viewers, especially impressionable young people, with the idea that there are not and never were any straight people who ever did anything of note, who ever contributed anything to history, or who ever even existed at all. But why should the producers or scriptwriters care about a little thing like that?

Immortals must fight each other for some obscure reason nobody understands. Typically lesbian. It may have something to do with the planet Zeist, but after all the television adaptations from the movies, nobody's sure anymore.

Moe is a "Watcher." She has a tattoo to show that she belongs to a secret society of mortals who know about the Immortals but are sworn to secrecy because—well, just because. Moe runs a little lesbian jazz club, and no straight person has ever come in there, either! Watchers devote themselves to keeping detailed records and photos of Immortals like Dyckan and young Bitchie Ryan the leather-jacketed motorcycle dyke, because—well, just because.

Immortals walk around packing cumbersome swords under their coats in case they are challenged. Whenever an Immortal comes anywhere near another one, they recognize each other immediately by a ringing in their heads. That's Immortal gaydar. Sometimes an opponent challenges Dyckan while she's at a lesbian festival, but they must postpone their duel since there is a law (nobody knows why) that they aren't allowed to fight each other on holy ground.

I am a Watcher, too. I watch Lowlander and wonder if, sometime, somewhere, Dyckan MacProud has ever met or is ever going to meet a straight person! Dyckan often has historical flashbacks triggered by her current circumstances. She is a good-looking, charming, sophisticated lesbian who has learned a great deal in 400 years. Naturally women, both mortal and Immortal, find her attractive. She also has integrity. Dyckan values life and does not like to kill, but does so when she must—which is usually once per episode—because there's another rule about Immortals that everyone knows (but no one knows why):

"In the End, There Can Be Only One."

That's okay with Dyckan; for many years she thought she was the only one anyway. But as a watcher, I can easily imagine how another watcher—someone with a different sexual orientation from myself, who is watching a show that claims to take a sweeping view of history yet is populated exclusively by those of my own sexual orientation—that other watcher might feel that something vital is missing from the picture.

Where No Dyke Has Gone Before

We are in bed. "Mmm," I say dreamily, still swirling in post-orgasmic bliss, "Let's do it exactly like that again soon."

"Un-hmmm," my lover agrees. She lifts her head drowsily off the pillow. "Computer," she calls out, "save program."

Later, when I phone some lesbian separatists I know, their answering machine tells me that I have successfully navigated Communication Level One, and I should leave a message. *"Once our computer has verified your voice, you will be advanced to the appropriate level of security clearance. Unless of course you are a Ferengi trader, in which case your call will be terminated immediately. Live long and prosper." Beep.*

Yes, I think elements of *Star Trek* have become firmly embedded in the Lesbian cultural positronic matrix.

But wait a minute. Here we have a future, progressive society where the people are so much more advanced—right? They've wiped out poverty, they've wiped out racism, they've wiped out most of the Earth's diseases, and they don't blink twice at aliens who have skin like slime and skulls like giant walnut shells.

So where are all the queers in the 24th century?!

Haven't they been allowed into the military *yet?*

The creator of *Star Trek*, the late Gene Roddenberry, promised that he was going to include some gay- and lesbian-themed material in future episodes of *The Next Generation*. Apparently his successors decided not to keep that promise. *Star Trek: The Next Generation* aired its final episode without so much as one openly homosexual character from this or any other planet.

No, I don't count that early gender-change episode when Dr. Crusher falls in love with a Trill man who turns out to be a symbiont, whose real crustaceoid self is living in his humanoid body.

After he dies it's implanted into a female "host" body—who is then rejected by Dr. Crusher because he's now a she.

And I certainly don't count the episode about the asexual Jinaii people, who reproduce by hatching out of fibrous husks. A few are "gendered" and hide it—one of whom (a female, of course) falls in love with Riker. They were trying to make a parallel with homophobia, I suppose—but the subtlety of the message reemphasized heterosexuality, since nobody at all was queer—the choices were heterosexual or nosexual.

Not only are there no lesbians and gay men anywhere to be seen on the Enterprise, but every dykey-looking woman on the show is required to demonstrate her heterosexuality. They usually end up sleeping with Riker, the default het hunk. What's worse, with the exception of the Jinaii, every humanoid alien culture they come across is fucking heterosexual!

I heard that gay scriptwriter/science fiction writer David Gerrold, who wrote the classic "Trouble with Tribbles" for the old *Star Trek*, did write a gay-themed episode for *The Next Generation*—and it was rejected.

So for all its progressiveness, *Star Trek* is still a world where no dyke or gay man has gone before.

If the producers of *Star Trek* were really going to make up for their egregious lack of lesbian and gay visibility before *The Next Generation* series ended, the synopsis of the "exciting two-hour series finale" would have read something like this:

When the Enterprise encounters a Lesbosian ship for the first time, Guinan realizes that her life's journey in pursuit of personal growth and wisdom must now take her to the ancient Lesbosian Star Cluster, where she will live among the advanced all-lesbian species for at least the next 500 years. When she cheerily announces this choice to Captain Picard, he becomes leery of the Lesbosians.

He also discovers that most crew members have been using the holodecks not to play detective as he has but to play out all their hidden homoerotic fantasies that have been suppressed by scriptwriters and producers during these seven long years of space flight.

Picard becomes still more disturbed when Counselor Diana Troi and Dr. Beverly Crusher ask him, as ship's captain, to officiate at their matrimonial union. They tell him that, influenced by the positive example set by the Lesbosians, they have finally decided to bring their long-term secret love affair into the open.

"But what will your mother say!?" sputters Picard.

"She'll just have to learn to accept it," answers the wide-eyed, determined empath Troi with a toss of her dark curls.

Meanwhile, Geordi and Data discover and explore some gay subroutines in Data's neural processors that Data's creator Dr. Soong wisely placed there for just such an option. Together they improvise a special thruster boost by hot wiring Geordi's visor to Data's induction coils.

When Picard confides his misgivings to Lt. Worf, Worf explains a little-known aspect of Klingon culture: "Among warriors, Captain, same-sex encounters are common. But as with all our mating practices, we Klingons do not discuss it—we *do* it."

Just as Picard is about to ban the Lesbosians from his ship, blaming them for the breakdown of proper military regimentation, they beam aboard former Enterprise head of security Tasha Yar, who tells the stunned Picard that she did not die attempting to escape from her Romulan captors, as everyone had thought, but in fact was rescued through the Lesbosian underground. She has been living freely among the Lesbosians ever since.

Yar explains that the ecological problem with warp drive can be solved: the Lesbosians use an entirely different technology—a safe, even faster method of interplanetary travel that will not cause toxic rifts in the integrity of space. It is called Astral Cliterodynamics.

The Lesbosians offer the Federation this new technology, and invite cultural exchanges for those advanced enough to appreciate the Lesbosian lifestyle. Picard assigns Ensign Ro Laren to be the first to participate in such an exchange, doing research among the Lesbosians; she eagerly accepts. Major Kira of *Deep Space Nine*, her earcuff tinkling, puts in a cameo appearance as the newly appointed Beijoran liaison to the Lesbosians. And Wesley, having become lovers with the Traveler while exploring higher planes of existence, arrives in time for Beverly's wedding to Troi.

After the ceremony, the Lesbosians, along with Guinan, Yar, and Ro, bid the rest of the crew goodbye. Riker walks the pensive Picard back to his quarters. "Well, Captain, what do you think?" Riker says in a low, confidential tone.

"About what, Number One?"

"Should we incorporate this new drive into our propulsion systems?"

Picard gives him a long look, then makes his decision. "Make it so," he nods. "Yes Sir!" says Riker, smiling, as he begins unbuttoning Picard's shirt.

We see the Enterprise glide beautifully off into deep space, for the last time—before the reruns.

Stay tuned for the Lesbosian Star Cluster spinoff series—mere decades away.

ART DYKO

What is love? 'tis not hereafter: Present mirth hath present laughter…
—Shakespeare, *Twelfth Night*

Treasure of the Lost Crocodykes

We tend to take it for granted these days that lesbians have a literary tradition that can be traced back at least as far as the Greek poet Sappho, who lived and composed superb love lyrics to women around 600 B.C.

But we wouldn't have been able to say for certain that she wrote poetry celebrating romantic love between women if it weren't for the Egyptians and their elaborate burial practices. And we owe a large debt of gratitude to some mummified crocodiles for unintentionally preserving our priceless lesbian literature.

For over a thousand years, Sappho's work was all but lost. Her reputation as the greatest woman poet who ever lived was sustained almost entirely by hearsay—through descriptions of it by other authors. The true story of how some of the lost treasure trove of her poetry was recovered reads almost like the plot of an Indiana Jones movie.

In January 1895, a young journalist mentioned the mystery of the lost art of Sappho of Lesbos in, of all places, the *Lincoln Nebraska Journal.* Perhaps not so strangely, it appeared in a column written by a precocious twenty-two-year-old writer named Willa Cather.

"There is one woman poet," Cather wrote, "whom all the world calls great, though of her work there remains now only a few disconnected fragments and that one wonderful hymn to Aphrodite."

In Cather's day, the *Ode to Aphrodite* was the only poem of Sappho's that one could read. It had survived simply because it had been quoted in its entirety in another work, *On Literary Composition* by Dionysius of Halicarnassus. He had quoted it as an example of poetry in its highest form.

The "disconnected fragments" Cather mentions were a few brief references—sometimes just a phrase or two from other poems by Sappho—that had survived in other classical authors' works. It was similar to someone today quoting a line from a Shakespeare sonnet—only in those days before motion pictures the written and spoken word carried a lot more importance. Every educated person in ancient Greece and Rome would have been familiar with Sappho's poems because they studied her work in school. She was so famous that coins were minted in her honor.

Scholars at the great library in Alexandria, Egypt, hundreds of years after Sappho's death, had compiled exhaustive collections of Sappho's work. Altogether they had about 1,200 verses that they believed constituted her lifetime output. They classified these verses—according to meter and subject matter—into nine separate books. Sappho's poetry was quoted, studied, analyzed, and referred to in the grammar books and rhetoric books of Greece and Rome to give students examples of great writing to emulate.

In Cather's 1895 column, she said that the few fragments and one poem left were "small things upon which to rest so great a fame, but they tell so much. If of all the lost riches we could have one master restored to us, one of all the philosophers and poets, the choice of the world would be for the lost nine books of Sappho. Those broken fragments have burned themselves into the consciousness of the world like fire."

Knowing more about her personal life in retrospect, one can speculate that "Willie" Cather had a particular reason to want to read the lost books of Sappho above the works of other philosophers and poets. But Cather wasn't overstating the case when she called Sappho's poetry "lost riches." The lost books of Sappho were not just "lost" as in misplaced somewhere, either. All nine collections of her poetic masterpieces had been deliberately destroyed.

When the first wave of destruction of Sappho's work occurred is not precisely known today, but it's believed to have taken place quite early in the Christian epoch, most likely during the period of Gregory of Nazianzus, about 380 A.D. The Christians, known for their zeal in defacing pagan monuments, can't take all the blame, however. The conquering Moslem general who entered Alexandria in the seventh century burned all the library books except the Koran as "unnecessary," and torched the great library over the weeping protestations of the librarians and scholars. A final great wave of the bookburnings that destroyed forever whole chunks of our world literary heritage took place during the religious fervor preceding the Crusades, in the time of Pope Gregory VII. In 1073

A.D. Gregory ordered the thorough and systematic persecution of the works of ancient authors considered "immoral," and these works were publicly burned in large numbers in both Rome and Constantinople at that time.

After these successive purges of uncounted thousands of pagan works, the *Ode to Aphrodite* survived, just by luck, thanks to that quote in Dionysius.

During the Renaissance, arguments arose about the use of the pronouns "she" and "her" in Sappho's one surviving poem, since it's clearly about love and desire.

In it, Sappho prays to the goddess Aphrodite to help persuade her lost lover to return to her, because her heart is full of anguish. There is no mistaking that Sappho is asking the Goddess of Love to persuade an unnamed "her" to come back—and that Sappho had called on Aphrodite in the past in similar circumstances with other women! Not men, but women!

Seventeenth century Greek scholars debated about whether or not "she" was a mistranslation. Since Sappho's work had been so thoroughly erased, it was still possible to argue that the romantic references to women in the Ode were clerical errors. These august scholars theorized that some bleary-eyed medieval monk—out of overwork or a perfunctory knowledge of the Greek language, perhaps—must have confused the pronouns when he transcribed Dionysius, inserting a "she" where the quote must have been a "he." This argument was, believe it or not, seriously put forth to explain the Great Pronoun Problem in reading Sappho.

There were plenty of other clues that hinted that maybe the "she" was not a mistake. Though her poetry was lost, a number of other quotes *about* her still existed. The pagan historian Maximus of Tyre (125-185 A.D.) had read all nine books of Sappho in the second century A.D., and he pretty much laid the cards on the table by comparing Sappho's interest in women with Socrates' interest in men: "What else could one call the love of the Lesbian woman than the Socratic art of love? For they seem to me to have practiced love after their own fashion, she the love of women, he of men. For they said they loved many, and were captivated by all things beautiful."

But that could be dismissed as hearsay. And heresy.

By the nineteenth century, the English poet Swinburne—who wrote with a lavender quill himself—commented that Sappho was "beyond all question and comparison the very greatest poet that ever lived."

But no more of her work had been found, nor was likely to be.

Here's where Indiana Jones comes into the picture, in the form of two British archeologists named Grenfells and Hunt.

In 1896, just one year after Willa Cather's column appeared, something truly remarkable happened. Her thoughts about finding the lost books of Sappho were so prophetic, one might conclude that the goddess of lesbian literature was listening. Grenfells and Hunt were excavating Graeco-Egyptian cemeteries at a place called Oxyrhynchus (Behnesa) in Egypt, when they stumbled upon a horde of ancient writings.

It turned out that the coffins Grenfells and Hunt were digging up were made of a kind of papier-mache. They discovered that scraps of ancient papyrus books and letters, torn into strips and pasted together, had been used to construct these coffins.

The ancient Egyptian people, you know, were very fond of mummification. They mummified sacred animals—bulls, birds, cats, dogs, monkeys, and crocodiles—in the same manner they mummified their pharaohs. In addition to the scraps of papyrus the coffins were made of, Grenfells and Hunt found that other papyrus strips had been wadded up and stuffed into the mouths of the mummified sacred crocodiles buried at the site.

The writings found on these scraps dated from the late second century A.D., and some of these crumbling pieces of newly uncovered, precious papyrus held the *only known copies in the world* of lost ancient masterpieces.

Among them were works of Sappho.

Do you realize what this means? The most important, earliest woman-loving literature, the foundation of our lesbian literary heritage as we know it today, lay buried in the sands of Egypt for almost two thousand years, little pigment marks on mashed plant matter crumpled up in the bellies and chest cavities of pickled crocodiles!

But here's where Indiana Jones bows out. Separating and restoring these crumpled, crumbling pieces of papyri proved to be painstaking work, and it was some 20 years before all the recoverable segments were finally published. As Sappho translator Mary Barnard explains: "Papyrus books were long rolls of a kind of durable paper made from the stalks of a water plant. The poems were written crosswise on the roll, in capitals because lower case had not yet been invented. The papyrus scrolls were eventually torn into strips, crosswise of the roll, lengthwise of the poem, and pasted together."

In effect, someone had ripped up some dusty old scrolls containing ancient writings that everybody knew at the time because they had lots of other copies lying around back then. This ancient equivalent of yesterday's newspapers just happened to include some of Sappho's poems. They were all torn into strips to recycle as coffin material and mummy stuffing for the sacred crocodiles!

I like to think that the sacred Egyptian crocodiles that were the guardian angels of our lesbian sacred texts, so to speak—the crocodiles we owe such a large cultural debt to—were *lesbian crocodiles*. Why not? They *could* have been.

Not everything was salvageable, however. Since all of these writings were recovered from torn strips of material, in some cases only the middles of each line could be pieced back together; in other cases, only the left side or the right side was found. This is why, when reading Sappho's poems today, brackets or ellipses are put in to indicate a part that is missing from the papyri from which the poem was recovered.

Altogether, about 600 lines or parts of lines were recovered by the archaeologists—remarkable, beautiful, and vivid. A real-life lost treasure found. One small sample:

Some say an army of cavalry, others say infantry
and some say a fleet of ships,
is the loveliest sight on the black earth;
but I say it is whatever you love

What we now have today is still only about five percent of Sappho's work, that is, five percent of the 1,200 lines in those nine books at the library of Alexandria.

But at least that much has eluded the destroyers. That five percent is about ten times more than there was a mere hundred years ago, when Willa Cather wrote her piece in the *Lincoln Nebraska Journal*.

And it laid to rest once and for all the notion that Sappho did not mean "she" when she said "she."

Yet even after the great discovery in Egypt, Sappho's *Ode to Aphrodite* is still the only *complete* poem of hers we possess. I love to think that, unlikely though it may be, there's more lesbian literary treasure out there, hidden in some desert tomb or island cave, waiting to be found. That next year or next week, more lost work of ancient lesbian writers will be resurrected from our silenced past.

Who knows? Perhaps an *entire set* of the nine books of Sappho has already been found, and it's nailed up, packed away and lying forgotten in some vast government warehouse, like the Ark of the Covenant found by Indiana Jones.

Part of a poem by Sappho
recovered from *Oxyrhynchus Papyri*

Double Vision

Last Tuesday night I was perched in my usual spot in the crow's nest of the opera house, watching the Chicago debut of John Corigliano's opera, *The Ghosts of Versailles*. A male friend and I have been going to performances at Chicago's Lyric Opera together for well over a decade. We have comparatively cheap seats high in the stratosphere of the opera house—the first row of the second balcony.

Through the years I have noticed that the visibility of lesbians in the opera audience grows in inverse proportion to the price of the seats. But it's not so bad in the stratosphere, unless you suffer from vertigo. You can hear the music very well—you just can't see the singers' faces onstage way below you without binoculars.

We were in the midst of Act One Scene 3 when I hurriedly nudged my friend to hand over the high-powered binocs. Cherubino (played by a woman) was courting Rosina. In a pastoral flashback scene, Cherubino coaxed Rosina toward the Temple of Love, singing:

> "Come now, my darling, come with me,
> Come to the room I have made for thee.
> Let us strew the bed with flowers—
> There we will spend the hours."

By that point I had the focus perfectly adjusted, and watched through the nine-power lenses as the pretty blonde Swedish mezzo Charlotte Hellekant lovingly met the eyes of the equally lovely dark-haired American soprano Sylvia McNair. As Cherubino and Rosina, they joined hands and pressed their bodies together. Rosina had been hesitant to yield to Cherubino's advances, but as he (she) caressed her, she replied, "Yes, yes, my darling, I'll come with thee..."

Together the couple sang: "Though hours pass swiftly, Love is eternal," as the voices of Marie Antoinette and Beaumarchais, watching onstage, joined them. Then Rosina and Cherubino kissed.

I wanted to jump up out of my seat and shout to everyone sitting calmly around me, "Do you *see* this? Two *women kissing* onstage!! It's not really a guy and a girl, it's two real live women!! Kissing!! Isn't it faa-bulous??!!"

I had to suppress this urge, of course, not only out of respect for the singers, whom I did not want to interrupt, but also because from the first row of the second balcony, with a hundred-fifty foot drop gaping before me, this kind of a sudden move could amount to a suicide leap.

Leaping lesbian joy from the opera balcony, inspired by two women in rapture onstage, has struck me a number of times before. Jokes about muff divas aside, a woman (usually a mezzo) playing a male role is hardly rare in the world of opera. But still it always gives me a thrill to watch.

Sometimes female characters are "disguised" as men as a part of the plot, like Leonora in Beethoven's *Fidelio*. That's kind of fun. Sometimes they play minor male characters. *Boris Godunov*, Gounod's *Faust*, *Don Carlo*, *Rigoletto*, and many other operas have parts written for women as young men, sons or pages of the king. Oscar, a leading role in Verdi's *Un Ballo in Maschera*, was written for a woman. The urbane, androgynous Count Orlofsky in *Die Fledermauss* is often sung by a mezzo.

Sometimes it's a romantic part, in which the mezzo makes love to the soprano. That's my favorite.

The romantic young Cherubino in Mozart's *Marriage of Figaro* is sung by a woman—and at one point, to add yet another twist, "he" pretends to be a girl. In Strauss's *Rosenkavalier* the Act One curtain opens to show two lovers, Octavian and the Marschallin, played by two women, in bed together.

Seeing the love duet in *Ghosts of Versailles* reminded me again of the most amazing musical experience of this kind I've ever had—the first time I had the impulse to jump up out of my seat and shout out, "Do you *see* this? Two *women kissing* onstage!!" It was a number of years ago when Lyric staged a little-known Bellini opera from 1830, *I Capuleti e i Montecchi*. All but forgotten in modern times, Lyric scored an artistic coup by rescuing this gorgeous opera from obscurity and bringing it back into the repertoire.

Bellini's *I Capuleti e i Montecchi*—the Capulets and the

Montagues—is the familiar story of Romeo and Juliet. What made it especially interesting to me, and unusual even for opera, is that the part of Romeo was written for a mezzo soprano—not a minor or secondary character, but the principal male role and the romantic lead of the opera.

There was a lot of hoopla over the opera's revival. A number of dedicated opera fans were flown in from New York just to see Lyric's production. The internationally acclaimed Greek diva Tatiana Troyanos was to sing the part of Romeo.

Of course, I expected that seeing two women play Romeo and Juliet—whose very names evoke the theme of love-against-all-odds—would be an interesting experience. Casting Troyanos as Romeo promised to deepen the level of realism in the part, though, since she had been listed in *Outweek*'s infamous roster of closeted celebrities during the magazine's controversial "let's out everybody" crusade. Knowing that Troyanos might be singing not only onstage but also in the choir added an extra bit of anticipation for a lesbomaniac like me.

But I was not prepared for Troyanos's startling entrance as Romeo in Act One. She appeared stage left looking as if she had stepped right off the dust jacket of Judy Grahn's *Another Mother Tongue*.

Talk about the Lavender Woman! She was a vision of bold romanticism. With her curly blonde hair cut to an androgynous length, she wore lavender boots, lavender tights, a lavender doublet with lavender sword sheath at her side, and a flowing lavender cape.

I had to think that Troyanos was making more than a fashion statement in this get-up. Someone—presumably costume designer Ulisse Santicchi—must have made a conscious decision to turn the female Romeo into the embodiment of the Lavender Menace!

Musically, Troyanos was superb. The part was technically demanding, and she sang it brilliantly. She played Romeo as a single-minded young lover, full of tenderness and ardor. Her duets with rival Tebaldo, and, particularly, with Juliet, were tempered to perfection. Italian soprano Cecelia Gasdia made her American operatic debut as Juliet, and portrayed her as a frail, ethereal girl, singing the part with great expressiveness.

In fact, Troyanos and Gasdia made the sexiest couple I've ever seen on an operatic stage. Their love scenes were intense, all the more so when I watched their faces up close, magnified. They were *believable*. They practically steamed up my binoculars; I don't think I put those heavy lenses down once during the entire performance. After the sizzling love duet in Scene two, it was not only possible but easy to see the entire story in a lesbian context. What were the quiet, attentive people around me thinking? I wondered. Were they just accepting it as operatic convention? It was hard to believe that they didn't get the subtext, since it wasn't being muted.

It took me quite awhile to stabilize my blood pressure after the tragedy ended. You just don't see this kind of thing at the opera! Even critic Bernard Holland, in reviewing Lyric's *Capuleti* for *The New York Times*, felt compelled to point out that "the two make an affecting pair on stage."

It was true—but what an understatement.

Several years after this singular operatic experience, Tatiana Troyanos, still very much at the height of her career, was diagnosed with cancer. She withdrew from performing to undergo treatment, but only a few months later, she died of liver failure.

A gay friend of mine who sings opera professionally now in New York tells me the opera dish from time to time. I asked him about the widespread rumors that Troyanos was a lesbian.

"Oh, yes, she was a lesbian all right."

"But she wasn't ever out, was she?" I asked. "I mean, *out* out. Officially."

"Well, maybe not *officially*," he said, laughing, "but she was about as out as you could get without wearing a rainbow coalition hat studded with pink triangles."

It's true. I saw it with my own eyes—aided by the binoculars. I'm glad I was here to see Troyanos as the Lavender Romeo, singing so gloriously in all her lavender finery on this very stage where the company of ghosts at Versailles, Marie Antoinette, Beaumarchais, Cherubino and Rosina, are now enacting their play within a play. Alas, wherefore art thou, Tatiana?

Full Metal Closet

If you were a lesbian in Medieval Europe, what would you do? The job opportunities were almost nil.

If you tended to the femme side, you would probably become a nun. In those days, when someone told a lesbian, "Get thee to a nunnery!" they didn't have to say it twice.

If the Church was not an option, marriage was usually impossible to avoid. You'd simply have to hope your parents would marry you off to a very old geezer and cross your fingers for an early widowhood. Or speed things along yourself, if you knew anything about Deadly Nightshade.

For those few in the upper reaches of society, a job as a lady-in-waiting for royalty might be just the ticket. If you could fend off the earls and dukes and other suitors, you could stay in private apartments in castles with the other ladies, and you wouldn't have to keep them waiting.

If you were rich enough, you could keep your own residence after you married and supplied your husband with heirs. That wasn't frowned upon—in fact it's still done today.

And of course, back when Knyghthood was in Flower, butchier lesbians could become knyghts in shining armor and simply carry their closets around with them. What could be a more thorough disguise?

The Medieval Code of Knyghthood said you had to worship a Lady and rescue her from other knyghts if she was a damsel in distress. Dykeknyghts had no problem with that. Not all of these Ladies they worshiped would have been lesbians—but most straight women were kept so ignorant of sex back then anyway that, like the modern jazz saxophone player Billy Tipton, a dykeknyght might even marry her Lady and the Lady would be none the wiser.

Or perhaps she was the wiser, and realized her good fortune—so she gladly held her tongue.

Knyghts were also supposed to go on quests. They were especially fond of looking for something called the Holy Grail. This Grail was an elusive jewel-encrusted cup or chalice, and if they could find it and put it to their lips, they would attain a state of ecstatic heavenly bliss.

No doubt many a lesbian knyght who went off on the quest for the Holy Grail found that elusive cup with no trouble at all, waiting for her under the covers of the warm bed of a local prioress.

And when a lesbian knyght was wounded in war or jousting, she really had it made, since it was common practice for knyghts to recuperate in one of the numerous secluded abbeys, where attentive lesbian nuns would use everything within the power of their healing arts to lovingly nurse her back to health.

But no matter what their station in life, lesbians back then knew that it wasn't safe to be openly gay.

Unfortunately, when the Age of Knyghthood began to wilt, most lesbians could no longer hide in their traditional places. But they couldn't just flip up their visors, flip down their codpieces and jump right out of their full-metal closets.

Joan of Arc had tried to live as an openly lesbian knyght, and she was burned alive in 1431 for repeatedly refusing to wear a dress.

That terrible incident was a wake up call for Everydyke.

Joan's was a valiant attempt at coming out, but it not only failed—it had blown everybody else's cover. Lesbians saw the writing on the castle wall. They couldn't hide behind hammered steel, or even black muslin, forever.

Sex in Medieval times was made purposefully difficult for all women to enjoy, with those many buttons and hooks to contend with, chastity belts, drafty bedrooms, and jealous husbands with battle-axes to worry about. Lesbians not only had a great deal of trouble finding one another under their disguises, but once they did, it could sometimes take hours to get out of those chain-mail suits and those voluminous layered nuns' habits.

But even though it wasn't safe to be out, once they climbed out of those pinching suits of armor and constricting robes, they began to feel better. More modern, somehow. Once they didn't have to wear all this creaking high-maintenance hardware, and they didn't have to wear these long, weighted black dresses with hoods that hid all their hair, they started to feel really terrific.

Knyghts no longer felt like a rump roast in a pressure cooker. And without those habits that cut off circulation to their heads, the nuns were rid of their migraine headaches.

That led them all to start thinking more creatively. It occurred to some of them that they could infiltrate the same territory that the gay men were flocking to in droves: the Art World.

Imagine what a bursting of energy when they all came Out! Going from full suits of armor and walking mountain-ranges to lounging around naked on pillows while gay men painted them. The sheer joy they felt exploded into a newfound sensuality. It was so much easier to have sex once they weren't wearing all those clothes! And the more lesbians took their clothes off, they realized, the more sex they could have with each other!

And that was the beginning of the Renaissance.

Art Dyko

During Late Gothic times, fat blonde lesbians were much in demand as artists' models in Italy and Northern Europe.

Artists painted fat women because plumpness was highly favored after the Middle Ages, when everyone had been starving. Lesbians were available to work during the day and on short notice. Lesbian models were less trouble than straight women, because they didn't usually have husbands who would come barging into the studio in a fury when they discovered their wives were standing around posing instead of working at home cleaning out the slops, milking the goats, and giving birth to baby number nineteen.

The great Renaissance masters—like Botticelli, Raphael, Tintoretto, and Parmagianino—used mostly blonde models because, even in southern Italy, paintings of the Virgin Mary sold better if she looked Northern European, though common sense would dictate that she be portrayed as Semitic. Ditto for the baby Jesus.

The fat blonde lesbian models were glad to get the work—even the ones who had to peroxide their hair now and then. As today, towns tended to be centers for the arts. It was easier for lesbians to meet in a big cosmopolitan center like Bruges or Ghent. And since artists' models were always ostracized for loose morals, they had a great excuse to hang around with each other.

Holding the same position for hours at a time could get tiresome. Still, it was a lot better job than being married with twenty-odd kids, and trying to juggle your time so you could sneak off to the local lesbian wayside inn for a few hours.

And being an artists' model was definitely preferable to being burned at the stake during the witch craze.

Fat blonde lesbian artists' models often gave helpful suggestions to the painters about how best to use light and perspective, and the artists valued their input.

One day, somewhere around 1450, some brilliant lesbian model, probably in Flanders, began to make suggestions about subject matter as well.

The market for paintings of the Virgin, she knew, was in a slump. The artist was depressed. The model really didn't want to lose such a good gig.

"Master Jan, a word if you please," said the model, whose name has not, alas, come down to us through history, but it might have been Miranda. "Methinks people have more than enough paintings of the Virgin already. Withal, the market be flooded."

"Aye, 'tis truth," saith the artist.

"And truth to tell thee," said Miranda, "'tis become very wearying beneath this blue veil, holding this blonde babe who crieth and peeith apace. Mayhap the public would favor some mythological themes as well? Mayhap Greek and Roman myths, like Minerva and Venus, or Athena and Apollo...?"

Many of the artists were gay themselves, and Miranda's classical mythology idea appealed to Master Jan. Most of the male models were also gay, and they liked her idea, too. They were tired of standing around in the itchy muslins of shepherds and carpenters.

By 1500, paintings that depicted themes from classical mythology had become increasingly popular. The plan worked so well that many more lesbians had been hired as models. There was more work for everybody, and the dykes were very happy to strike poses looking mythologically at each other. Marry, but 'twas a bold plan! They could be visible and invisible at the same time!

Lesbians were also responsible for the innovation of nakedness in these new classical-themed artworks.

A lesbian in Italy who was modeling as Venus turned to the artist and said, "O Maestro Piero, a word. Why shall we not remove more of our clothing, per che? Surely the goddess of amore was not so bent over with gabardines? And, ecco, methinks that way your paintings will sell more quickly, tanto presto."

Maestro Piero—who had been wracking his brain trying to come up with a way to sell more art to the nouveau riche—realized she was right. "Bennissimo!" he agreed.

As the artists became more and more successful and market-driven, lesbian models continued to suggest daring liberalities in portraiture. The Renaissance was, after all, a time of sensual reawakening.

"Methinks, Master Lucas, that perhaps three of us together, naked, would be even more fetching?" suggested another lesbian innovator.

"Gadzooks, what brilliance!" exclaimed the artist.

"And Lucas, my dear, I beseech you. Suppose I put mine hand behind me and nudge Britomart slyly in her darling sparrow's nest?'

"Whither?"

She put the back of her hand against another lesbian's vulva. "Thither."

"Ah, yes!" saith the artist. "But then what shall the lady on your right?"

"Mayhap lovely Amoret could lift her foot so that her dainty little toe brushes mine own sweet nether pudding? For symmetry and balance?"

"Odds Bodkins, that's subtle! Ladies, prithee hold that pose!"

As the craze for art works of naked women accelerated everywhere, throughout Italy, Belgium, Holland, Germany, France, and England, the lesbians continued to suggest new, ever more sexually provocative poses.

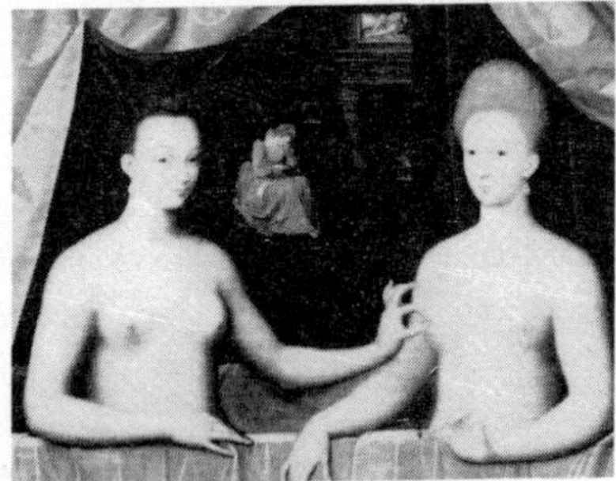

"Mayhap my lovely Giselda and I could stand naked from the waist, our arms out just so, and I most daintily pinch her incomparably supple nipple, thuswise?'

"Forsooth, what artistic perfection! I beseech thee, ladies, hold that pose!"

And as time went on, the lesbian models got even plumper. Since there often still were food shortages, fat was appreciated more than ever. The models were happy, healthy, and ate far better than the women who worked their fingers to the bone for their husbands. They stood still most of the day, and got less exercise than if they were plowing fields and skinning hides. If the painter was a fast worker, they could all feast on the bunches of grapes, fowl, rabbit, fruits, vegetables, and cakes he had arranged for his still lifes.

Fat lesbians began cropping up everywhere in art as the

Renaissance evolved into the Baroque—in Titian, Giorgione, Reubens, Rembrandt. And it is in the art of the Baroque that we see the tradition of the fat blonde lesbian artists' model reach its full flowering. Naked fat lesbians giving each other the eye, grabbing each other's love handles. Half-dressed lesbians lounging on sofas or out in the woods, waiting for their lovers to arrive. Clothed fat lesbians in huge gowns, squeezing each other and playing footsies.

Dykes understood what a good thing they had going. It was nice work, and they could get it. They could stand around touching each other with no clothes on for hours. Often in these pictures they weren't even supposed to be giving each other come-hither glances, but the artist captured that dykey look between them on his canvas.

Of course, there was a downside. Holding highly intimate poses for long time periods would tend to be frustrating as well as arousing. They passed the time whispering sweet nothings to each other.

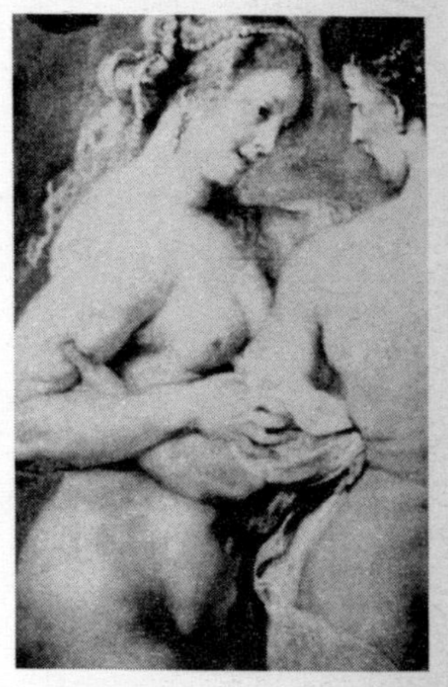

"A thousand kisses would I lay on thee, could I but have thy body hence," one naked dyke would whisper in another's ear, while grabbing her, as they both stood still as statues.

"Oh," her naked companion would respond softly, "I pray thee, hold not back thy ardor, but pour out thy most cherished longings to mine eager ear..."

After several hours of this, the models' increasingly labored breathing would probably necessitate a break for a pint of frothy ale.

"Egad, Pieter, we are weary," the models would say. "Prithee respite us, and sally forth to work on that landscape thou hast labored over this fortnight? Take Helmut with you, ere you need company. We shall take our ease here and await thy return."

That gave the artist and his boyfriend a perfect excuse to go frolic in the woods. The dykes had plenty of time to curl up together in the studio on a bearskin rug with soft swansdown pillows, where, once alone, they could release all the pent-up sexual energy they'd accumulated from two or three hours of naked proximity and whispered lovey-talk.

As time went on and they got more bold in their lesbian escapades, the risk of exposure increased. But these dyke models cleverly avoided detection.

Since nobody took women seriously, they decided to deliberately perpetrate the myth of the dumb blonde. Then, important men in the world of commerce who came into the artists' studios would pay no attention to the models, except to gape at them. These powerful men would speak openly, thinking the women didn't understand. In this way the lesbians could keep their networks informed of political and social intrigues, and keep abreast of was happening.

And if people became very suspicious of the bohemian ways of the gay artists and lesbian models, they could marry each other and allay any rumors.

The subtle lesbian content of Renaissance art had definite subversive value. Ornately framed, ready to hang on a wall, lesbian imagery could slip into the home of a wealthy burgher disguised as an item of furniture. And there it would promote lesbian culture, as the patron's marriageable daughter could stare at it at her leisure, wishing she might join the revelry of these carefree women of wild abandon in the woods. Or slip next to another as she languished on her satin cushion.

Back in those days, the secret sign lesbians wore to recognize each other was not the labyris pendant but the pearl drop earring. The pearl and the drop seemed to them to be appropriate symbolism for lesbian love.

You can tell simply by looking at Renaissance and Baroque art how many of the models in these paintings were dykes. Even in a seemingly heterosexual theme like Venus caressing Mars—really a lesbian model caressing a gay male model—those pearl drop earrings let you know that it's all a pose.

If you look today on the walls of any major museum of the world, you will see fat blonde lesbians smiling on their couches, some dressed, some undressed, some holding their breasts, gazing fondly at each other, grabbing each other vigorously, and some boldly staring out from the canvas—innocently, seductively, mischievously, invitingly—directly at you.

Leon or Leona?

For almost five hundred years people have been staring at the Mona Lisa, wondering about the riddle of her smile. Leonardo da Vinci's painting of this unknown Italian woman is the most famous portrait of all time. Kings, emperors, art lovers, and practically everyone who looks at it are drawn to the mysterious smile playing about La Gioconda's lips. But nobody ever seems to notice the equally mysterious riddle of her cleavage.

About ten years ago an article appeared in a number of newspapers and magazines claiming a new discovery about Leonardo's celebrated painting. Computer scientists had analyzed Mona Lisa's face. They had come to a startling conclusion: if you factored in certain variables for age and sex, the proportions of her features matched Leonardo's own portrait as an old man. In other words, Mona Lisa was a self-portrait of Leonardo himself, as a *young woman*. I'm not kidding.

Everyone had supposed there was a real woman who was the model for the Mona Lisa, but nobody could pinpoint who she was. There was no record of her, or of anyone having commissioned the piece. Leonardo kept the painting with him always, continuing to work on it from time to time. He was obviously very fond of it. He took it along with his other personal possessions when he left Italy, and it was still in his studio when he died in France in 1519, at the age of sixty-seven.

The computer finding was a bombshell at the time. What could it mean? Was it a split personality thing, like Glen and Glenda? Was that why the many notebooks of Leonardo were written backwards, so you have to look in the mirror to read them? Did Leonardo like to wear women's clothing? Did he want to be a girl?!

As far back as 1916, good old Sigmund Freud had proposed a theory about Leonardo's sexuality. Leonardo's biographers up to that time had avoided mentioning the strong possibility that

Leonardo had been gay. To give Freud begrudging credit where credit is due, he was the first writer about Leonardo who was willing to discuss the sex life of the great Renaissance genius.

And what Freud proposed was that Leonardo didn't *have* any sex life. Yes, he had definite homosexual impulses, Freud admitted, but had probably never acted on them. In his famous *Leonardo da Vinci: A Study in Psychosexuality*, Freud says Leonardo was a "homosexual in feeling," but not in practice. That he "restricted" himself to "so-called ideal homosexuality"—"ideal" meaning not that it was perfect but that he kept it in his head.

Freud believed Leonardo was "homosexual in feeling" because his mother must have showered him with too much love while his father was not around. Freud based this supposition on two items of evidence: the fact that Leonardo's biological mother, an unmarried peasant woman, raised him till he was five (after that, he lived with his wealthy father and stepmother), and a childhood dream Leonardo mentions in his journals, about a vulture that wiggles its tail in little Leonardo's mouth. Freud was certain this was symbolic of breast-sucking changing into penis-sucking, which Leonardo promptly suppressed anyway.

Freud's conclusion, in a nutshell, was that Leonardo's libido had been stunted in a stage of infantile sexuality because of the excessive love his mother must have shown him. It doesn't seem to occur to him that peasant women might not have a lot of time to fawn on their children. Plus, no one really knows much about Leonardo's mother—she could have beat him every day with a stick for all Freud knows.

But according to Freud, Leonardo lived most of his life in this repressed sexual state, sublimating his erotic feelings into art works of genius. Until one fateful day, when Leonardo was in his fifties, and a young married woman of a prominent family from the town of Gioconda walked into his life wanting to have her portrait painted. Her beautiful smile—and Freud has no evidence whatsoever to base *any* of this fantasy on—"awakened in him," Freud says, "the memory of the happy and sensuously enraptured" smile of *his mother!* "This unlocked the great well of repressed feeling" in him, and he painted her face with its blissful maternal smile not just on his portrait of her, but on every face he painted for the rest of his artistic career.

Freud's study of Leonardo's sexuality is a case study, really, in how heterosexuals like Freud can turn the lives of even creative gay geniuses into dreck for Hollywood movies. Picture, say, Sean Connery as the aging, bearded, lonely Leonardo, and Demi Moore as the young matron with the winning smile from Gioconda.

Of course today we are more attuned to gay realities. But aside from the dream Freud found so revealing and the bare facts about his origins, the clever doctor had a number of other clues about Leonardo's life at his disposal:

—Leonardo had been a beautiful male model for other painters in his youth. (His face is identifiable in a number of works by other Italian masters.)

—He loved to dress in magnificent, expensive clothing.

—He was well-spoken, mild-mannered, well liked and "appreciated every refinement of conduct."

—He hated war and bloodshed. He was a vegetarian who didn't believe in killing animals, and he loved to buy caged birds in the market and set them free.

—He wrote that the "act of procreation" disgusted him.

—When he became a master painter, he took as his pupils "only strikingly handsome youths." Not a one ever became a prominent artist.

—He was left-handed.

—Oh, yes, and by the way, he'd been *imprisoned as a young man for homosexuality.*

Apparently it never occurred to Dr. Freud, the father of psychoanalysis, that the great Leonardo might have "evaded everything sexual" in public because he'd already been *arrested* and sent to prison once, and knew how lucky he was that he managed to get acquitted!?

I guess the great Viennese doctor never heard the famous psychological maxim, "Once imprisoned, twice shy."

Freud never even entertains the likelihood that behind the closed doors of Leonardo's studio, he and Francesco Melzi—the painter who started out as an apprentice and lived with Leonardo *for the rest of his life,* the man who travelled everywhere with him, the man Leonardo *willed* all his property to when he died—had been lovers!

I was in Paris last fall, and I visited the Louvre with several of my lesbian friends. While we were there, we decided to check in on Mona Lisa. I'd seen her in person before, fleetingly, when I was young and she was on tour at the Metropolitan Museum in New York. I saw her in the Louvre once before, too, but that was years ago, long before I'd heard about the new possibility about her/his "secretive" smile.

This time I wanted to look carefully at her face to see for myself if Leo looked back at me.

There are 300,000 art works housed at the Louvre, but it's easy to find Mona Lisa. Signs all over point to her, and once you enter the enormous hall of European painting, all you have to do is look for the spot where people are crowded around the velvet cordon five or six deep, staring intently at what's probably the most valuable 1.2 square meters of canvas in the universe.

My friend Dolores and I each took our turn to absorb her image. I got as close as I could. I looked carefully at the smile that's been variously described as fascinating, perplexing, enchanted, enigmatic, radiant, indecipherable—an unsolvable "riddle."

"It's definitely him," Dolores said as we stood there, other tourists pressing around us.

"You know, I think it *is*." Mona looks as if she really wants to break out into a grin, but she's suppressing it. You can almost see the muscles on either side of her mouth moving slightly, tensing and releasing, making an effort to keep from smiling more widely.

"The theory used to be that she was smiling like that because she knew she was pregnant and hadn't told anyone."

"It's his little joke on straight people. And what a good one."

If it's true, it's a joke on that great sexmeister Freud in particular.

"They did an x-ray scan on it once," I said, "and found a string of pearls around her neck, but Leonardo painted them out again."

"Well, how typically gay-drag," said Dolores. "Can't decide whether to wear the pearls or not."

"You know, something about her breasts looks really strange. Look where the cleavage line comes at the top of her dress. It's up way too high and too far to the left. It's practically in her clavicle.

"Not only that. I never noticed it before, but she's basically flat-chested. She's just got this roundness, but it's a pushed up kind of roundedness. There's a definite cleavage line where there's nothing there to cleave."

"No wonder it looks so strange," said Dolores. "It's not anatomically correct."

Now, Leonardo probably had the most extensive knowledge of the human body of anyone in the Fifteenth Century. He personally dissected dozens of bodies and made anatomical drawings from them that are still admired today for their scientific accuracy.

I let my eyes wander back and forth between that smile and the cleavage line. It seemed to be saying to me: Anybody who simply has eyes to see can tell that my breasts can't possibly be real. "That's why she was having trouble suppressing the smile."

Maybe she's even imagining all the millions of people in future generations who will look at her breasts in puzzlement.

"God," said Dolores, "he was such a genius."

"Really. And an inventor. I wonder if he knew that some day we'd have computers that would be able to piece together the two faces, and we'd stand here realizing we should have noticed the male breasts all along."

"Oh, I think he knew exactly what he was doing."

I started thinking about Leonardo's other masterpieces. *The Last Supper:* Thirteen guys sitting at a long table at the very moment Jesus says, "One of you will betray me." You could see why such a theme would resonate for someone who had already been jailed once for being gay.

Just across the wall from Mona Lisa is Leonardo's *John the Baptist*. Art critics have always commented on how androgynous he looks. Freud mentions this, too—and how his smile resembles Mona Lisa's. In fact, he almost looks like Mona Lisa in a curly wig. "He's pointing his index finger straight up, as if to say, 'If you want to know why I'm this way, don't ask me, ask the Big Guy upstairs.'"

The Louvre also owns Leonardo's *The Virgin and St. Anne.* Freud himself noted something peculiar in that one, too: even though the picture, also called *The Holy Family,* is supposed to depict the baby Jesus with his mother and grandmother, both women look about the same age. Freud's explanation for this is that Leonardo was imagining his real mother Caterina, and his stepmother, Donna Albiera, who would have been about the same age, when he painted it.

But what was he imagining? It's true that the two radiant, smiling women look just about the same age. But in addition to that, one woman is sitting on the other woman's lap!

"Maybe Leonardo's mother and stepmother had an affair while his father was away." Or maybe Leonardo had some deep psychological longing for a gay family unit.

"Look at the expression on Anne's face," I said. Anne gazes down at Mary's neck like a woman in love, and with her elbow out boldly, as if she'd like nothing better than to pull Mary, who's leaning down, back up, and say, "Let the kid go play with his pet lamb for a minute and kiss me, you fool."

Look at the paintings again sometime—preferably in person, and preferably with gay and lesbian friends along—and you'll see for yourself. Check out Leonardo in his Mona Lisa drag of course, but don't miss Mary and Anne, either. Leonardo was so far ahead of his time that he painted the Holy Family—the ideal family unit—as a couple of very happy lesbian moms with their kid.

One of these days I'm going to browse again through the facsimilies of Leonardo's notebooks filled with sketches and designs of his many invention projects, because I bet somewhere among them is a mechanical prototype for the first turkey baster.

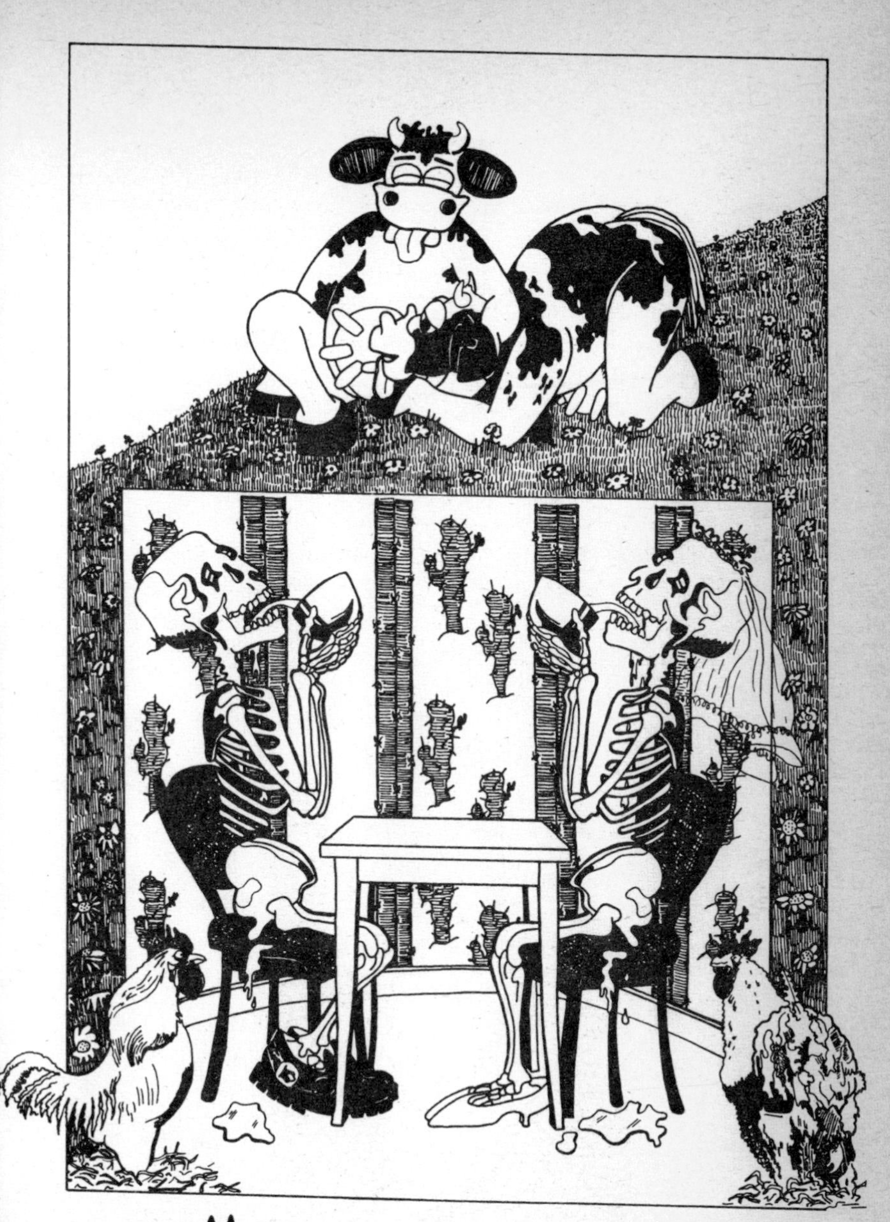

valley of the phobes

Making an effort to be normal, that's what it is to be colonized.
—Nicole Brossard, *The Ariel Letter*

Reliable Dykumentation

Sometimes it pays to eavesdrop on straight people who are talking about gays. Especially when it's gossip. You may learn something you didn't know.

Conversation overheard at a restaurant. Two decidedly straight-looking couples in their mid-twenties on a double date:

"Oh, Keanu's definitely gay, but he had to say he's straight," said the male half of Couple A.

"They've gotta do that," Male of Couple B said, nodding. "They know in Hollywood that their careers would be over. Their credibility would be shot."

My dinner partner and I had stopped our own conversation to listen to this one. I rolled my eyes. She rolled hers. We've heard this argument a hundred times through the years, and it's always seemed absurd. From the mouth of someone straight, it seemed slightly offensive and condescending at the same time.

I mean, really. Credibility? Who *believes anything* they see in the movies anymore?

The big blockbuster movies don't want to confuse anyone with anything remotely believable. People went to *Batman* to see what all that special effects money was spent on. Whoever went to *Waterworld* went to find out what on earth could have cost so much. Personally, I've gotten so jaded about the entertainment business that when a train crash or a big explosion is shown on the screen, my immediate thought is, 'I wonder how much *that* scene cost to make?'

We eavesdropped some more.

"Yeah. Like, the audience doesn't want to know they're acting during the love scenes," said timid Female of Couple A.

I'm biting my lip at our table. Oh—like in *Prince of Tides*, for example? You see Barbra Streisand playing a psychiatrist, and Nick Nolte playing an unemployed high school football coach. You know perfectly well that in real life she's not a psychiatrist and he's not a high school football coach. There's no way you can look at them up there on the screen and forget who they really are. If the producers were seriously concerned about credibility, they'd hire unknown actors, whose faces no one knows, so we wouldn't be so distracted by their celebrityhood. Plus, we've already been bombarded with publicity about how much money they got paid to play the part, we know who they brought with them to the film's opening, we've been dished out anecdotes about what went on during the making of the film...

From the standpoint of credibility, it's a wonder that a big star in a film doesn't *ruin* that film for the audience. So this credibility argument can't be based on disrupting the dramatization. It's got to be based on the notion that some people may not like them anymore solely because they are gay. And that's homophobia pure and simple. The one thing that *must* be assumed is heterosexuality.

"John Travolta. He's definitely gay, too."

"But he's married," protested Female B.

"That doesn't mean a thing," said Male A.

At our table, we smiled and arched our eyebrows.

"He's into scientology."

"Oh really, is he? I didn't know that."

Is that true? I whispered. My companion nodded.

"Definitely," Male A said, nodding. "All the gays in Hollywood are into scientology."

Sure, I whispered, *What is it, a genetic link?*

"Really?" said Female B, skeptically.

"Well, not *all* of them," he corrected himself. "But a lot."

But L. Ron Hubbard was a major homophobe, I whispered across the table.

My companion shrugged.

"Scientology is a front for gays to meet each other in Hollywood, and to find people they can marry."

My companion and I stared at each other in wonderment. As

much as everyone likes to speculate about what famous people are in the closet these days, the McCarthyist undertone of their conversation didn't seem to occur to these people.

"And k.d. lang is a lesbian," said Female A.

"Uh-huh. But she's a really good singer."

But?!! I was ready to turn over their table.

"And Melissa Etheridge, too," said Female B.

The fellows didn't seem to know about her. How they missed that one, I don't know.

"But she's really sexy."

But?!!

"A friend of mine's been in a couple of movies, and he told me Richard Gere is gay."

We sighed.

"And Tom Cruise."

"Really? I wonder what Nicole Kidman thinks about that," giggled Female A.

"Is she into scientology, too?"

"Yeah, I think so."

Could this possibly be true?

"And Paul Newman is gay, too."

That stopped us both short. My companion got a quizzical look on her face.

"He married Joanne Woodward so they could cover for each other. She's gay, too."

"I've never heard that before," said Female B.

Neither had we.

"Oh, yeah, he's gay. So is she. Everybody in Hollywood knows it."

Couple B and Female A remained unconvinced.

"Look," Male A said, "if they aren't gay, how come they've stayed married so long?"

There he had us all stumped.

It would take a straight person to come up with such an insightful commentary on the state of modern marriage.

Fear and Loathing on Long Island

In the community there's a lot of discussion lately about the damaging effects of shame on the lesbian and gay psyche. I'm sure it's true. But me, I can't recall ever having much shame about my actual desire to have sex with women.

Fear, definitely—fear of other people's reactions if they found out. Of being made fun of. Of being thought of—if not treated—as something repulsive. Of seeing female friends' faces become horrified that I might interpret their affection "that way." Of being physically endangered by homophobes.

These kinds of fears are well-founded in the reality of our experiences. We've had to put up with this kind of shit for as far back as we can remember. And then maybe these fears turn into shame like some sinister feedback loop.

And everyone gets piled up with *some* shame from our Judeo-Christian tradition about anything sexual in general. Expulsion from the Garden of Eden and covering our nakedness and conceiving children in sin, and all that. But I began questioning biblical doctrine at a pretty young age.

Once I began to think about lesbian sex, I didn't see why there would be anything *more* shameful about sex between two women or two men than there was about sex between men and women. It was just different *kinds* of sex.

I came Out to myself comparatively late, so maybe I missed consciously feeling "wrong" about being a dyke because as a teenager I was so self-conscious about everything else that was "wrong" with me. I was fat and kind of bookish. I was a working-class kid who went to an upper-middle-class high school, so the kids on my block thought I was social climbing while the kids at school pitied me for being so culturally backward as to prefer Phil Spector over Béla Bartók. And I was (so my mother put it) "too smart for my own good."

In my "straight" days, if I felt wrong about anything sexual, it was my embarrassment and puzzlement that I just didn't enjoy sex with men very much, but felt some social pressure to act as if I did.

So pow, when I came Out, I shouted "Vive la Difference!" and became a born-again lesbomaniac.

For years now I've been Out to just about everybody I know. And yet I had never quite managed to tell my parents. Fear of rejection rearing its ugly head again. They were down on me for so many other things—starting from way back in my hippie days—that I could just hear my mother saying something like, "It wasn't bad enough you dropped out of college? And you hung out in the Village with all those beatniks?! Now this?!"

It was easy to rationalize not telling them. They lived on Long Island, a thousand miles away from Chicago. I saw them very infrequently. We were on polite terms but hadn't been close in years anyway. Blah blah blah. Why not just leave well enough alone?

But when my father died, I found that I wished I had told him. If for no other reason, to really know what his reaction would have been. To give him the benefit of the doubt that he might have been more open-minded about my lesbianism than I ever gave him credit for.

I decided I'd tell my mother, even if she disowned me or told me she never wanted to talk to me again.

At least she couldn't say, "Don't tell your father, it'll kill him."

So the next time I visited her, I came Out to her.

Her initial reaction was surprisingly philosophical. She said: "Well, it's sick and disgusting, but if it makes you happy, what do I care?"

This was better than I'd hoped. I was very encouraged. We obviously had a long way to go before we'd be in agreement about the subject. But it was a good start. Because somehow, despite all her own homophobia, she'd recognized immediately the possibility that being a lesbian might actually make me happy.

"But," she said, sighing, "It's a good thing your father never knew about this, because it would have killed him."

Animal Crackers

I tried to convince my mother logically that being gay was neither sick nor disgusting. I found that this method had limited success. But then who ever said homophobia is rational?

Actually, my mother had a gift for baffling people so completely with her logic that she could bring a conversation to a total halt.

For example: My Aunt Ella, my mother, and I were having coffee one day, several years ago, talking about how much the world had changed since I was a kid.

My mother turned to me. "Do you remember Teresa Norris's mother's second husband?"

Teresa was one of my close childhood friends. "No, Ma, I don't. I don't even recall Teresa having a stepfather."

"You probably don't remember him because they weren't together very long."

"Oh no?"

My mother sat up in her kitchen chair as her indignation rose. "Well, the one thing he wanted Teresa's mother to do was to iron his shirts. And she wouldn't do it. So they broke up."

My mother waited for our reaction.

Silence. My aunt and I looked at each other.

I didn't know where to begin trying to figure this out. My mother could not be trying to prove that Teresa was screwed up by a broken home, because Teresa turned out to be a great person that everyone admired, raised by her mother and grandmother. So what could it be? Was my mother suggesting that the stepfather was gay? A dandy obsessed with starched shirts? Or that he made no sexual demands on his wife and that was bad for their marriage?

"He didn't want her to do *anything* but iron his shirts?" I asked tentatively.

"That's right." Now the indignation fairly crackled in her voice. "It was the one thing he wanted her to do. And she wouldn't do it!"

Finally Aunt Ella said gently, "Well, Helen, there must have been more to it than that..."

My mother looked at my aunt with utter contempt. "Well," she said angrily, as if Ella was a fool, "then why wouldn't she iron his shirts?"

My aunt and I looked at each other again, and couldn't think of another thing to say.

Once we had bridged the subject of gay and lesbian matters, my mother was open to discussion, but only up to a point. "Where would we be if nobody had children?" she asked me abruptly one day.

My mother complained often that there were too many people on the planet now—certainly way too many shopping malls in her area alone. So that was an easy one.

"Ma, there are 100,000 people born every week. There are five billion people on the planet right now."

"Isn't that awful?" she said.

"And anyway lots of gay men and lesbians *do* have children."

"Isn't that awful?" she said.

"What do you mean? Is it more awful than too many straight people having children?"

"Well, no. They all stink, as far as I'm concerned." She sighed. "But I've heard enough about all this gay and lesbian stuff. I don't want to hear any more about it now."

I sensed I had reached the level of her tolerance. "Why not?"

"Well... because it's unnatural, that's all."

"But Ma," I said, "Any farmer will tell you that it *is* natural, just as natural as heterosexuality."

Now, I know from nothing about farms, but a friend of mine who's married to a farmer told me that, word for word.

"I have a friend who's a farmer's wife, and she said lots of farm animals are gay, too."

"So," my mother said without missing a beat, "you wanna live like an animal?"

Going by the Book

Lesbians have complained to me at dyke Halloween parties when I've shown up in regular street clothes: "You aren't wearing a costume!"

"Yes I am," I'd say, and I'd point down to my feet.

I wear the same thing every year: Over my motorcycle boots, I slip on a pair of huge, ugly stretchable latex feet. These feet have big ugly gnarly toes with jagged broken toenails, and lots of hot pink synthetic hair on them. They go up as high as my ankles, right over my boots. The top part of each foot forms two pink hairy straps that fasten with velcro at the back so they don't fall off. I found them at a Woolworth's—in the Halloween stuff aisle—a number of years ago. Ever since, that's what I wear to celebrate the Autumnal Equinox. No muss, no fuss.

"Ugly feet? What kind of a costume is that?"

I'd strike an imposing stance, and shake the fluorescent pink tufts of hair on the latex feet that add what is, to my mind, that special queer touch to the overall effect. "I am a Lesbian Bigfoot," I'd tell them proudly.

Okay, I know, you're supposed to wear a *costume* costume to a Halloween party. I've always loved Halloween, and when I was younger I used to spend a lot of time and thought dressing up for the occasion. But being a simple Lesbian Bigfoot has a lot of advantages. After the party, I don't need any cold cream to wipe off gobs of makeup or other itchy crap stuck to my face, and if that 31st of October happens to be a chilly night, I don't have to freeze all the way home in some flimsy cheesecloth nightie thing. I simply unvelcro my pink-haired feet and, like the "real" Bigfoot, Lesbian Bigfoot has vanished in a flash!

Bigfoot, you know, is the North American continent's version of the legendary Abominable Snowman of Mongolia. This rarely-glimpsed humanoid roams the wilderness of the Rocky Mountains as the equally seldom-spotted Abominable Snowman roams the high mountain crags of the Himalayas.

Everybody's used to my costume by now. When I arrive they say, "Ah, here's Lesbian Bigfoot!" Of course, I never win any of the prizes for best costume at the Autumn Equinox parties. Nor do I expect to. But what most people don't immediately appreciate about my Lesbian Bigfoot costume is the concept: it's an outfit with biblical connotations. Because as an Abominable Snowperson, I am abominable. I am an abomination.

Now let me say that I respect the Hebrew Bible (what Christians call the "Old Testament") and the New Testament as historical accounts of the spiritual thinking and social practices of the peoples who revered these texts, and as expressions—often very beautiful expressions—of the creative imagination of the people who wrote them. I've particularly read the Book of Leviticus, the Hebrew book of laws, a number of times because that's the Bible chapter homophobes always cite in their condemnation of gay people. In the King James version of the Bible, the one I grew up with, Leviticus condemns sex between men as an "abomination."

The word "abomination" comes from the Greek, "ab-hom" meaning "against man," as in subhuman. That's how the Abominable Snowperson got his/her English name, too. In Asia they call him/her a Yeti.

Leviticus says some very good things: that you should respect your elders, don't steal, don't lie, and don't cheat. Lesbian Bigfoot and I both do try to live by these rules. But Leviticus also includes a hefty list of "abominations," and if you do certain things, that's what you are. Some of the rules make a lot of sense as a guide for desert nomadic peoples living four thousand years ago—but are not necessary today, unless you wish to strictly follow the letter of the ancient Hebrew laws. For example, eating leftovers after three days makes you—not to mention your stomach—an abomination. Well, they didn't have refrigerators in ancient Galilee. If you developed a canker sore or a rash, you'd have to stay away from people and bathe carefully before you'd cease being "unclean." Today we have penicillin.

Other abominations have to do with how the ancient Hebrews

distinguished themselves from other groups in custom and habit. A person who wore the ancient equivalent of a Beatle haircut, for example, would be an abomination. But I know that today there are members of the Christian Coalition who wear bangs—I've seen them on television. To sport some styles of beards—the unHebrew kind—would also make a man an abomination. Anyone who had a tattoo was an abomination. If you wore garments made of two different materials at the same time, you were also an abomination.

That means that every preacher today who condemns homosexuality in a wool-blend suit is just as much of an abomination as the gay people he is condemning.

The Hebrew Bible actually has very little to say about men who have sex with each other—but they, too, were an abomination. But gay stuff is very minimal in Leviticus—two brief mentions. At least ten times as much space is devoted to condemning adultery than male homosexuality.

The punishment for some abominations is to be stoned to death. Gay men do fall into this category. So do adulterers. As far as adultery goes, I can think of a few preachers and politicians who, if they really believed what they were preaching, would have to go stand under an avalanche. And if Christians and Jews really adhered literally to the laws of the Bible, they would stone rapists to death, too. That might not be so terrible. But they'd also have to stone their victims to death in exactly the same way. If some Bible-thumping TV evangelist's daughter was raped, I doubt he'd want her stoned to death along with the rapist—but that's what the Bible plainly stipulates. And according to Leviticus, it doesn't matter whether the rape victim is a woman, a man, a child, or an animal. Everybody must get stoned.

The point is that homophobes have latched on to the two one-sentence mentions of gay sex in the Bible as some kind of ironclad condemnation. But they themselves will ignore other equally binding or far more binding Biblical laws whenever they consider them to be archaic, or barbaric, or simply inconvenient.

And contrary to what some rightwing religious leaders and politicians lead people to believe, the Hebrew Bible is completely silent on the subject of women sleeping with women. As a woman, if I were to take the Bible literally, I would never sleep with men, but only women. "Thou shalt not lie with mankind as with womankind. It is abomination," it says, right there in Leviticus. Okay, then I shalt not. The Bible tells me so.

And if you really want to be a stickler about it, line for line, the Bible has a lot more anti-family sentiment than anti-gay sentiment.

Lesbians and gay men do get a one-line condemnation in the New Testament, in Paul. But there's not one word in the teachings of Jesus that condemns homosexuality, either. It's all a lot of trumped up hatemongering.

What the Bible stresses over and over, chapter after chapter, verse after verse, is the importance of being honest. As a group, lesbians and gay men do an impressive job of being honest in the face of the jeering mob. But most of the Christian Coalitionists among that mob will never give us credit for that.

That's why I like being an abomination at Halloween. But of course all the little children going trick-or-treating on a pagan holiday are abominations, too. Since the Bible doesn't say lesbians are abominations at all, I'm not an abomination as a lesbian. I'm an abomination because when I'm masquerading as Lesbian Bigfoot, I'm wearing latex, synthetic fibers, and velcro. The Bible has nothing more specific to say about latex and velcro than it has to say about penicillin or refrigerators, but mixing clothing materials is a specific no-no. An abomination.

Remember that you are disobeying the explicit Laws of God as handed down to Moses the next time you put on a cotton/rayon/nylon shirt, or a bra or a girdle, or a spandex jumpsuit. And you're in danger of transgressing the next time you pull that old cold pizza out of the fridge to zap it in the microwave. The next time you get a haircut. In fact, if you go strictly by the Book, just wearing a pair of canvas-and-rubber tennis shoes is a far worse offense than being a lesbian, since—Holy Moses!—being a lesbian is no offense at all.

27-YO GWF Seeks VHSBMW

The Personals. The Yuppie-Guppie-Luppie Love Connection. Maybe she'll hit the lottery and find the woman of her dreams.

So she pours herself a glass of white wine, relaxes on the leather sofa, and scans the ads. She finds one that—well, maybe it's fate or intuition, but everything about it sounds like a perfect match for her:

Feminine woman, 27, seeks same. Petite non-smoker. Successful entrepreneur on her way up the ladder to success. Want to join me in life's adventure? My friends tell me I'm cute and have a good sense of humor. Spiritually-minded, warm, honest, and caring. Enjoy theatre; Mozart. Love walking in the park, and soft candlelight dinners followed by nights of dazzling amour. No opportunists, no mind games—been hurt once too often. Woman of my dreams, are you out there? Please respond! Thoughtful, intelligent, open minded. No butches, no bisexuals, no schizzos.

She is excited. It sounds like just the person she's looking for!

She responds to the ad.

She discovers to her embarrassment that the ad was placed by her own recent ex-lover, whom she never wants to see again in her life.

She is hopping mad. She goes back and reads the same ad again. This time she can read between the lines:

Feminine woman, 27, seeks closeted lesbian. Prefers corporate executive high-roller who will move me into her condo where I can quit my job and live rent free in exchange for ultramodern non-monogamous, no-strings-attached sex that will inevitably fade into undisguised neediness on my side and excruciating boredom on yours. Poor self-esteem, tacky dresser, bad habits, negative charisma. Lots of ambition but no talent, no real goals, overly sensitive, slightly paranoid, suspicious of everyone, cranky. Desperate for attention. Several shallow but well-placed acquaintances. Enjoy faking multiple personality disorder for sympathy; will tolerate Mozart but prefer Yanni. Very low libido, but find big price-tag gifts momentarily very sexually arousing. Any race, any sign, depending on income. Drinker, dope-smoker, you name it, just don't act queer. I'll end up hating you no matter who you are. Whips and chains OK if you supply toys and pick up at least one of my Visa bills. No butches, no butches, no butches.

She is angry, but she is also pragmatic. She decides that her ex-lover's ad was a good marketing strategy, since she herself was prompted to respond to it. It just couldn't deliver the merchandise—it was false advertising. Hoping someone just like herself will respond, she places an ad herself. It is the same ad, word for word, as her ex's original published ad—except for the last sentence, which now reads: No bisexuals, no schizzos, and definitely *no narcissists.*

My lover Kathy called me at my mother's house. She had driven in to visit some old friends in Manhattan the same week I was visiting my mother out on Long Island—just a two-hour drive away.

"Would you like to meet Kathleen?" I asked my mother.

I had told my mother about Kathy by then, but she'd never met her. She'd never met any of my lovers.

"No," she said emphatically. "I have enough friends already."

My mother did have a lot of friends. Now that she was widowed, Ma had turned into a salon hostess for seniors. She had people trooping in and out all afternoon, mostly her neighbor-lady friends, and they'd sit around the kitchen table chatting and laughing and sipping glasses of port wine. It wasn't exactly the Michigan festival, but these seventy-year-old ladies seemed to be having the time of their lives.

Just about the only person my mother was not happy to see at the door was her own sister, Ella. She and Ella had been feuding for years.

My aunt Ella and my mother jointly owned the little house Ma lived in, and Ella and my uncle sometimes stayed there for the weekend. My mother was always thinking up little household improvement projects, and at some point she thought the curtains in my aunt's bedroom were dingy, so she made new ones.

"But did she thank me?" my mother said to her cronies. "Not her. When she saw the new curtains she said she was perfectly happy with her old curtains, thank you."

My mother's lady-friends listened sympathetically, as they sipped their wine. "If she thinks I'm trying to take over her bedroom, she's sadly mistaken."

It became their favorite topic of conversation. Every time my mother got into another fight with Ella, she couldn't wait to call me up to tell me about it. She had gotten a bee in her bonnet about my aunt.

"Ella was always ungrateful," she said. "When she was seven, she insisted on getting a pair of Ginger Rogers pants. And we couldn't afford it. But she got them anyway, because she was the baby..."

Well, that's families for you.

Anyway, my mother was even less enthusiastic about seeing my lover than she was about seeing Aunt Ella.

I didn't see any reason to push it. Ma was elderly. She had just recently become accustomed to the idea that I was a lesbian. Meeting my lover would be like having to really *see* me being queer. It would have been awkward for her—and maybe embarrassing, too, if she had to introduce Kathy around to all her lady-friends.

Kathy and I were going to meet at my alma mater, Stony Brook, about twenty-minutes from my mother's. She'd drive out in the afternoon, we'd stay at a motel, and then we'd have the next day together before she had to go back to the city. I arranged things so I could catch a bus to the campus from near my mother's place, since Ma was so adamant about not meeting my paramour.

As I was leaving, I wondered if Ma had told her buddies at the kitchen table, Mildred and Mary, where I was going overnight. "Bye, now," they all waved cheerfully. They didn't seem to care where I was going. They were all absorbed in their port wine, and in the latest dish about Aunt Ella.

"And last week, Mary, you know what she said to me...?"

"And I told her..."

"You know what you should say to her, Helen? Listen—this'll really get her..."

She and her cronies were having a great old time thinking up things to do or say that would be irksome to my aunt.

Actually, my mother was not thrilled with the idea that I was going to be gone overnight with my lesbian lover, but she went along with it—as long as I didn't give her any details. Unlike me, Kathleen was far from uppermost on her mind.

And Kathy wasn't eager to get in the middle of my wacky family situation, either. We both knew that she would have been a bit much for Ma and her friends. Kathleen was Out-and-a-Half. She wore buttons with lesbian slogans, she loved to create gay civic disturbances, and the trunk of her car was always brimming with gay and lesbian newspapers and flyers.

It was Coming Out Week at the university, and Kathy and I were in our element there. We watched *Before Stonewall* in the cafeteria. We met the gay man who was running for Homecoming Queen. We went to several other events sponsored by the school's Les-Bi-Gay group—which had just started up when I was a student.

Then we went off to a relatively inexpensive little motel in nearby Port Jefferson. Before we checked out next morning, we left a "Silence=Death" sticker on the Gideon's Bible in the dresser drawer.

Kathy and I were getting along splendidly. We drove around and went out to the beach. Long Island Sound was beautiful, the beach was misty and almost deserted, and seagulls were gliding silently.

Then it was getting late, and I called my mother to tell her that I was on my way home. "Should I have Kathy drop me off down the corner by the bus stop, or is it okay if she drops me off right at the driveway?"

My mother thought a second, then said, "It's okay if she comes up to the house. But why don't you just take the bus back?"

"Because she's going to give me a ride."

"But why should your friend"—she had yet to grant Kathy the status of a name—"drive all the way out here just to drop you off?"

She sounded cranky.

"Because she loves me," I said.

My mother didn't say anything.

Between the beach and my mother's house Kathy stopped at a farm stand to buy some grapes, and I bought a pumpkin and a bouquet of pretty purple gladiolas to placate my mother's bad mood.

"I'll tell her these are from you," I said, "so she'll feel guilty that she wouldn't meet you."

But as we arrived and I was getting out of the car, my mother, favoring her bad ankle, came hobbling all the way out to the driveway gate, making a fuss.

At first I was afraid something was wrong. Or even that she wanted to shoo Kathy away. "What's she saying?" Kathy called to me tensely.

I leaned my head back into the car and shrugged. "She says she wants to know if you'd like to come in for a sandwich!"

What on Earth...?

Kathy and I looked at each other in astonishment. But we'd stayed so long at the beach Kathy was already late to meet her friend in Manhattan.

"No, Ma, but thanks anyway." Kathy and I kissed right in front of my mother, and then she said goodbye and waved to me and my mother as she drove off.

I brought in the pumpkin and the bouquet of gladiolas. "Kathy gave me these for you."

"Oh." My mother was pleasantly surprised. "That was very thoughtful of her. She didn't have to do that."

Mildred and Mary were there in the kitchen—in pretty much the same spot they'd been the day before. They clucked about how nice it was, too.

"I know she didn't have to. She's a nice person, very thoughtful. I think she felt a little bad that you didn't want to meet her."

"Well, gee," my mother said, "I didn't mean to hurt anybody's feelings..."

I sat down at the table and joined the senior circle.

I discovered that my mother's real motive for inviting Kathy in was to ask her to run an errand to the liquor store. Ma and her lady friends had been sneaking shots from my uncle's bottle of Inverness scotch that she knew he kept in the back of Ella's bedroom closet, and they wanted to replace the almost empty bottle before he and my aunt arrived that evening.

"What's your friend's name?" asked Mildred politely.

"Kathy." I had no idea if they knew exactly who my "friend" was.

"She's a nice-looking girl, isn't she? What's her nationality?" My mother and her friends always asked about nationality.

Here was my inroad to talk about Kathy at last. "She's Irish. Her last name is O'Malley. And she was born on St. Patrick's Day."

"Well!" my mother said, putting the gladiolas in a vase. "Can't get much more Irish than that!"

"Irish!" Well, all the ladies liked that. Mary—who had been my mother's friend for fifty years, and her next-door neighbor for twenty—was Irish. Irish was always a plus. So I neglected to mention that Grandpa O'Malley was the only Irish in Kathy's family—she was one-eighth Irish and seven-eighths Czechoslovakian.

They asked me more questions about Kathy, and naturally I tried to put a good spin on my answers, but tactfully, in case my mother hadn't spilled the beans.

Another round of port wine among the ladies, and my mother had warmed rather a lot to the idea of meeting Kathleen. "You know," she offered, "the next time you visit, if you want to bring Kathleen with you, you can."

I was flabbergasted.

"Why not?" she said gayly. "You don't have to go to some motel. There's plenty of room here. The two of you can stay in your Aunt Ella's bedroom."

"Why not?" echoed the other two ladies, giving me a conspiratorial smile.

Why not indeed?

"I'm sure your Aunt Ella wouldn't mind!"

And there was general laughter round the kitchen table.

Momentary Glitch

"What's your computer password?" says my boss.

I am juggling my time between writing and graduate school and working part time. My job is in a nice suite of offices in a fancy glass and chrome skyscraper. In our office, we each have our own password to secure access to the database.

My boss looks at me expectantly. She is on the phone with the computer technician, Robby.

"You really want to know my actual *password?*" I say, a bit surprised.

A password, as you probably know, is a kind of sacred, secret, small word that you decide on, and you don't reveal to anyone. When you type your personal password in on the keyboard, it doesn't even show on the screen. And it has to be something simple—in this case five or six letters—that you can easily remember.

"Robby says there's a glitch in the whole system," my boss explains, the phone still up to one ear, "and he needs to go in and erase everybody's passwords one by one. And after he gets them all out and fixes the glitch, then you'll just have to enter a new password—you can't use the old one again, of course."

She waits, ready to spell aloud over the telephone my secret, private little word that nobody was ever supposed to know but me.

Had I been in the closet, I would have a sudden, silent panic attack at this juncture. I can't lie and make up a different word, because the computer technician has to know the right one. I am on the spot. Kind of like Lucy Ricardo caught in an embarrassing mess with Ricky.

But I *am* out at this job.

"It's L-E-S-B-O," I say.

"Okay, Robby? Here's Jorjet's password: L-E-S-B-O. That's

right, L-E-S-B-O. Sharon, you're next; what's your password?"

Nobody in our office is embarrassed—we all find it mildly amusing. My boss isn't a lesbian, but nevertheless she has read my book *Lesbomania*, and told me she enjoyed it.

After she has gotten everyone's passwords to the computer technician, and hung up the phone, my boss smiles at me, shakes her head and says, "You really are a lesbomaniac, aren't you?"

"Yes, I am," I say, "But I guess maybe Robby didn't know that till now. First time I've been outed by a computer code."

We laugh. It is a minor incident, but it reminds me how the closet works, and how awful it is not to be Out. What incredible amounts of energy, of man-and-woman-hours, must still be expended, day in and day out, for covering up, keeping a lid on that little secret, thinking ahead about where or how you might be 'exposed'! And the tension, when you never know who might find out, and tell who, and get you in trouble, or get you fired.

If I were in the closet, I wouldn't have even used a password that hinted at anything gay in the first place. That's the way it is in the closet—covering your tracks, as far back as your fear will make you go.

From my perspective, the benefits of being Out far outweigh the worry, the self-censorship, the awful feeling of not being able to express who I am—all the tensions that go hand in hand with closetude. I don't envy anyone who isn't Out, for whatever reason.

But I think everyone has the right to make these choices individually, depending on their situation. I don't teach high school in a small town in Mississippi, for instance. Or in Malaysia. I don't depend on some homophobe to approve my mortgage. I realize there are still many situations where people really can't be out without losing their jobs.

Speaking of jobs—where was I? Oh, yes. Typing in my password. L-E-S-...

Oh, wait, I had to change it, didn't I?

Typing in my password: D-Y-K-E-S.

Ah. Everything's working again, and I'm back in the system.

Family Outing

"Hello?"

"Hi, honey."

"Oh, hi Ma. How are you?"

"Oh, I'm alright. But you know what, I'm getting so forgetful. This afternoon I called up Mrs. Cunningham because she said she would take me shopping. I called her up and said, 'Hey, what about our trip to the store?' And she said, 'We went. This morning.'"

"You'd gone?"

"Yeah! And I just didn't remember! Isn't that something!?"

"Ma—Did you have any wine today?"

"No-o-o! Well, just one glass with Mary."

"You know, Ma, you really have to stop drinking."

"I am. I decided today, after talking to Mrs. Cunningham. I mean, that's embarrassing."

"Okay. That's good."

"And you know, I was thinking. Maybe next summer you and I could go together to Sunken Meadow."

Pause. "What?"

"You know, the annual family picnic. The picnic we have every year at Sunken Meadow State Park."

Pause. "You've never invited me before."

"All your cousins will be there..."

"Gee, I haven't seen them in years now."

"I know."

"It would probably be really nice to see them all again. But, you know, Ma, I'm not going to lie about anything."

"Lie?! Who's asking you to lie?"

"Ma..."

"Well, we don't have to talk about anything we don't want to talk about."

"Fine. I won't volunteer any information. But I mean it—I won't lie. If they ask me a question about anything, I'm going to tell them the truth. Okay?"

"Oh, so what's the big deal? They all know about you already."

"They do?"

"Oh, yeah. Sure."

"You told them?"

Pause. "Well, yes."

"When?"

"Last summer."

"Last summer?! You didn't tell me you told them."

"Well, I didn't know I did."

Uh-oh.

"What do you mean?"

"Remember I told you that when your cousin Johnnie went on vacation about a month ago, he came over to bring his dog so I could watch it for him while he was gone?"

"Yeah, I remember you telling me you were dog-sitting."

"Well, while he was here dropping off the dog, I made him a bowl of pea soup and we got to talking about you. And I thought, what the hell, why shouldn't I just tell him?"

"Wait, I'm already confused here. This is last month you're talking about now?"

"Yeah. I thought, what's he gonna say about it? If he doesn't like it, so what?"

"Well good for you."

"Yeah. So I told him, I sez, 'You know, Johnnie, Jorjet's a lesbian.' And he sez, 'Oh sure, Aunt Helen, we all know that.' "

Pause.

"Hey, Ma—Don't look at me. I know you didn't want me saying anything and I didn't tell him. I haven't talked to him at all."

"Oh, I know. He said I told him!"

"You told him."

"Yeah! He said that last summer at the annual picnic in Sunken Meadow—you know he was gonna drive me out there, and he was late coming to pick me up. And Mary was here and I guess we had a couple of glasses of wine before he got here…"

"Yeah…Go on."

"Johnnie said that I was feeling pretty happy in the car. But when we got to the picnic, I got out of the car and kind of slid down to the ground. I guess it was muddy or something…"

"Oh no."

"Yeah! And I couldn't get up again…"

"Oh no."

"…And while I was sitting on the ground waiting for your Uncle Henry to help me up, I just shouted, 'Hey, you know what?' …and then I kinda made a general announcement that you were a lesbian."

Pause.

"They were all there already, Johnnie sez. So that's how they found out. But you know, I don't remember anything about it. Isn't that something?!"

"Ma, now they probably all think that me being a lesbian is driving you to drink."

"Oh no-o-o, they don't. You drove me to drink when you were a kid. They all know it's your Aunt Ella who's driving me to drink now. Anyway I'm not going to drink anymore. So how about it? Want to come to the picnic next time? It's really a very nice family outing…"

Valley of the Phobes

I was in the hallway of my apartment building just putting my key in the door on the way back in from walking my dog. One of my upstairs neighbors, a newly-arrived immigrant from the Philippines, was on his way downstairs with his small son. The little boy saw my dog and came rushing forward to pet him. My dog, Spyke, is afraid of children and their quick, unpredictable movements. So I picked Spyke up and held him, just in case he was tempted to nip at the little boy out of self-protection. As I was holding him, he growled at the kid.

The little boy was frustrated that Spyke wasn't being friendly to him. He yelled back angrily at my dog, "You faggot!"

This boy is three years old. My dog is an eighteen-pound cocker-spaniel/pomeranian mix. Although neither this small child nor this small animal could have formed a cohesive concept in their minds of sexuality of any kind, hostility between boy and dog had somehow managed to take the form of homophobia.

Obviously the three-year-old could only have the foggiest notion of what "faggot" means. But just as obviously, he had already learned that it was a word he could employ when he was angry, as a put-down.

The boy's father continued on down the stairs—it was no big deal to him—and the child trailed after him. Leaving me with the faint stench of homophobia they'd deposited at my doorstep like a sulphurous fart.

Well, you could say, so what IS the big deal? It was just another one of life's little moments of ludicrousness.

Here's the big deal: only a week after the three-year-old called my dog a faggot, a gay man I know was attacked by three teenagers. He had just been walking down the street, minding his own business. They gashed his face with a piece of wood that had a nail on the end, shouting at him, "You faggot!"

Big trees from little acorns grow.

Of course I'm not saying that my little neighbor boy is guilty of a hate crime. And his father and mother have always been polite to me. But somebody close to that little boy has taught him, at a tender age, that "faggot" is a word he can use to lash out with. He's not even old enough to have heard it at school.

The notion that any of my neighbors may be offhandedly saying hateful homophobic things behind closed doors is creepy to me. And worse, it's the realization that these almost throwaway forms of homophobia can be such nonspecific, pervasive pollutants in the general atmosphere.

I mean, if my cocker-spaniel can be a faggot, then whatever you don't like can be a faggot. The guy who overcharged you at the garage. The absent landlord. The nasty lady at the ticket booth can suddenly become a big old bull dyke.

A faggot doesn't even have to be something living. Your shopping bag that unexpectedly rips on the way home from the department store can be a faggot. Your flat tire can be a faggot. Anything frustrating to a three-year-old can take on that little angry word as an all-purpose substitute for "damn it," "shit," or "fuck you."

It's a vicious cycle that's not limited only to anti-gay hate, but that seems to grow like weeds in the Valley of the Phobes. You use a word you've learned that puts down a group of people to express your small frustrations. At that point it's almost random, nothing to do with anyone who's actually in that group—just a convenient way to channel angry feelings. Then later on, a child learns to associate that hate word with a person or a group when he finds out there are specific people who can be called by that very word. And so frustration and hostility can come back to crystallize on a group of people when it started out as anger about something else—or about the world in general.

Now, I love being a dyke. And I love the word dyke. Very upfront and forthright word, to my mind. Though phrases like "fuckin' dyke" have been shouted at me in hatred, that only serves to make me more proud of my dykehood. And I know that some gay men feel the same way about "faggot."

I also know that there are some lesbians—mostly in the generations older than mine—who can't hear the word dyke even today without pain, remembering the times someone screamed it at them, or said it threateningly—sometimes while attacking them physically. It's been used too many times in a pejorative sense for them to be able to embrace it for themselves.

But changing that cycle of hate—and warding off self-hate—by refusing to accept the hate word as a hate word has been very important to the lesbian and gay community. I had a friend named Andy, an African-American pop and blues singer who performed locally in the early 1980s. His stage name was Christopher Street and he wrote openly gay songs. Andy was the first friend of mine to die of AIDS, more than a decade ago. I remember sitting with him at a bar in town called His N' Hers, talking about what kinds of strategies people use against name-calling.

"I got a harassing phone call just the other day," Andy said. "Some stranger calls me up and yells over the phone, 'You suck dick, you faggot.' And I said to him, 'You bet I'm a faggot. And you're a fool. You know why? You're throwing your money away to the phone company, Fool, just to call me up and tell me something I already know.'" Then Andy hung up on the anonymous caller.

I'm glad that as a movement we've reclaimed the words that have been used against us—faggot, dyke, queer, gay, lesbian. I see it as a kind of recycling project, kind of like cleaning up the air. Or like picking up the garbage people have thrown out at us, dusting it off and using it constructively. Some straight people wonder why lesbians and gay men feel the need to form their own communities. Well, for one thing, the air is cleaner there. We can breathe a bit better when we aren't in such close proximity to the toxic waste of homophobia down in the valley.

Sometimes subtle forms of hate can be such nebulous pollutants that you don't know how to locate their source or eliminate them from the atmosphere—but you need to do something because they keep stinging your eyes and your lungs. In the Valley of the Phobes there's an awful lot of hate pollution hanging in the air. It could, if left unchecked, slowly raise the acceptable level of hatred, and the fumes could eventually poison the social atmosphere entirely. The air—including the airwaves—here in America still has quite a bit of a stink to it in some places, wafting from several directions. And there are still a number of sites that are openly burning toxic heaps—like the ones emanating from the vicinity of politicians like Jesse Helms and Pat Buchanan. Every Anti-Hate Crime bill that passes a legislature is a kind of social Clean Air Act.

Cleaning the air of hate messages is a civic service that the general public may not yet entirely appreciate. There will always be disagreements between neighbors, and there'll always be a few skittish dogs who don't love children. But if we can keep up recycling efforts so they make headway against vicious-cycle efforts, we may be able to transform the Valley of the Phobes into a Valley of Friends that's a healthier place for all of us to live.

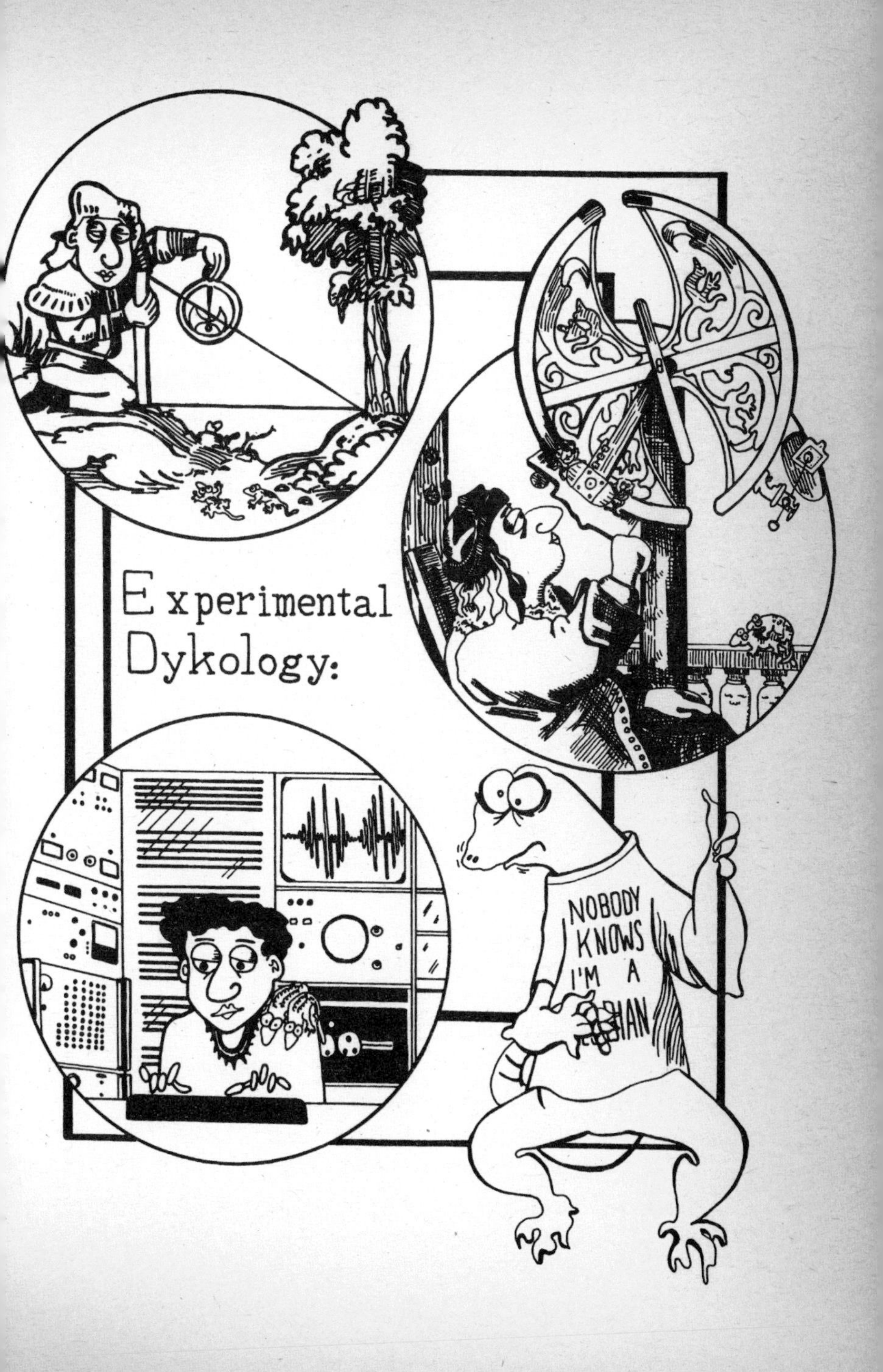
Experimental
Dykology:
NOBODY
KNOWS
I'M A

Let a man get up and say, "Behold, this is the truth," and instantly I perceive a sandy cat filching a piece of fish in the background. Look, you have forgotten the cat, I say.

—Virginia Woolf, *The Waves*

Testing, Testing...

While scientists painstakingly tease apart microscopic pieces of brain tissue to determine if there is any physical basis for gay behavior, several simple, easy-to-perform "tests" for being gay have surfaced in the last few years.

I found out about one such test on TV, on the *Murphy Brown* show. The FYI crew were trying to determine if a good-looking new consultant was gay. Corky Sherwood told her co-workers about the Shoe Test: If a man looks at his heel by lifting his leg sideways under his face, he's straight; if, however, he lifts his foot by bending his leg back and up, and looks down at his heel over his shoulder, he's gay. They tried several ways of tricking this young consultant into looking at his heel, but couldn't succeed in making him do it.

It turned out that he *was* gay, but they didn't discover it through the test. He knew what they were trying to find out, and as he was leaving the office, just before the elevator door closed, he said to them, "...and yes, I am gay."

I haven't tried this test on any of my gay male friends, so I don't know how well it works, but I can picture lots of high school kids surreptitiously trying it out on their classmates after that show was broadcast.

A lesbian friend of mine claims to have an accurate test for whether or not a lesbian is butch or femme—the Fingernail Test. You say to a lesbian, "Look at your fingernails." If she turns her palm toward her face and bends her fingers in to look at her nails, she's butch. If, on the other hand, she turns her palm away from her face and spreads her fingers straight to look at them, she's femme.

In my experience, the Fingernail Test coincides with a lesbian's butch/femme identity about fifty percent of the time—and if it's right half the time and wrong half the time, statistically it doesn't work at all. Often this test is used simply to make mischief: to embarrass butches into "proving" that they are femmes, which usually has the desired effect, since most self-identified butches detest being perceived as femme. I've even seen one butch insist on taking the test again, once she knew the "right" answer.

Often the test is tried on lesbians who say they are neither butch nor femme, to coerce them into admitting they are one or the other. That doesn't usually work, either, since the test itself is so suspect. Except for one outcome: if the woman you are testing punches you in the nose, says, "Fuck you," and refuses to look at her nails at all just because you told her to, you can be fairly certain that she's a butch. Even if she's straight.

Leafing through a recent issue of the unscoopable *Weekly World News*, I found yet another "test" for gayness—this is the Fingerprint Test. One of the riveting stories for which this publication is famous carried the following headline:

Shocking revelation is making headlines around the world!

YOU CAN PICK OUT GAYS BY THEIR FINGERPRINTS!

According to this article, you can "find out if your friends, coworkers or loved ones are homosexuals in two seconds flat" by simply comparing fingerprints of their left and right index fingers. If the left index finger has more lines and ridges than the right, "there's a good bet he or she's a homosexual."

This test works "equally well for men and women" according to a Dr. Robert DuPont, who, the article says, is a "famed French expert on human sexuality."

Dr. DuPont claims an "amazing accuracy rate" of 80 percent. "But in two of 10 cases, it is dead wrong." He says that the test has "far-reaching implications" that suggest homosexuality is genetic. "This knowledge could lead to greater understanding and compassion for people who are currently viewed as perverts by society at large. On the down side, the test has enormous potential for abuse. For example, businesses that routinely fingerprint job applicants could identify and refuse to hire homosexuals. And that is a grim prospect indeed."

Since the *Weekly World News* often prints stories with a decidedly anti-gay slant (I clip those for my "Homophobia" file), I thought this last comment was unusually enlightened for them.

But could this simple test be *true?* I ran to my desk and got out my rainbow ink pad and a sheet of white paper, and took the test myself. Under my magnifying glass, it appeared there were more ridges on my right than my left—*uh-oh*—the *opposite* of what the test said. But then I reread the directions and realized I'd tested on my thumbs rather than my index fingers. I did it again—getting purple ink smudges all over the paper. After several imprints, I finally got ones with the proper amount of ink to see the sworls and ridges on my index fingers.

Although they looked pretty much alike, lo and behold, the little lines were definitely a bit closer together on the left one than the right! And there were a few more sworly looking ridges on the left, too. Though I was still skeptical about this so-called test, I got a curious sense of satisfaction out of having "passed" it!

At last, "scientific proof" that I'm a dyke!

I confess that as a right-handed lesbian I'm especially fond of my right index finger (the same body part Holly Hunter's husband castrated in *The Piano*) and it has gotten a disproportionate amount of use over the years. I examined its contours. Perhaps my right fingertip has less ridges because they've worn down with time? But I decided that didn't make sense: While I suppose prolonged motion could conceivably wear a finger's tiny ridges down, it couldn't make them spaced further apart—could it? I don't think repeated motion has pruned down or obliterated any taste buds from my tongue, either.

Clearly, the 'gay fingerprint' story warranted further research. That weekend I brought the *Weekly World News*, my ink pad, and my magnifying glass to a party. I showed the article to the people there, mostly gay and lesbian, and a lot of them were game to try the test, too.

Surprisingly, despite the dubiousness of the source, most testees were actually willing to believe the test could work.

Afterwards, opinions differed depending on the result. Most of those who "passed" the test were inclined to think it might be true, while those who didn't were certain it was nonsense.

One straight man who "tested gay" didn't seem particularly upset at the outcome, nor did one gay man who "tested straight." But some lesbians seemed inordinately anxious beforehand, nervous that they might not "pass."

"What does it mean if I don't have gay fingers...?" one dyke moaned, staring at her hand.

The lesbians whose fingers didn't match the article's description tended to be disappointed or even indignant that the test said they "aren't gay." A few of the butchier women who "passed" the test seemed very pleased with themselves—even relieved.

In one case, a woman had slightly closer ridges on her right index finger, but more sworls on her left, so the outcome was split. "I guess that makes sense," she said, "because I'm bisexual."

So—to report the overall results: In this experiment, testing 25 individuals, we did NOT get an 80 percent match between fingerprints and sexual identity—in fact it was less than 60 percent. Therefore the "test" is not "proof" of anything. Like the other tests devised so far, it's mere modern folklore, and inconclusive.

If at some future time someone—at a job interview, for example—asks you, "What's that you have stuck to the bottom of your shoe?" then says, "What's that on your fingernails?" and asks you to give them a print of your index fingers, you can save everybody a lot of time, and just say "...yes, I am gay," and smile, like the charming young man on *Murphy Brown*. Or, if you'd rather, instead of giving them a fingerprint, just give them the finger. Middle, not index.

Species

There is a species of lizard called *Cnemidophorus uniparens*, commonly known as the desert grassland whiptail lizard. The natural habitat of this little critter is the southwestern U.S. and Mexico. What makes the whiptail lizard noteworthy for lesbian studies is that she reproduces by parthenogenesis—that is, without any male participation. In fact, there are no males among the whiptail lizards at all. Not one. Zip. It is an all-female species.

A study of these lizards, and some speculation about them as well, was published in the April 1987 issue of *Discover* magazine. While science is of course predicated on objectivity, the title of the piece, "Does pseudosex enhance virgin birth?" will alert the reader at the very outset to some potential cultural bias in the world of animal sex research.

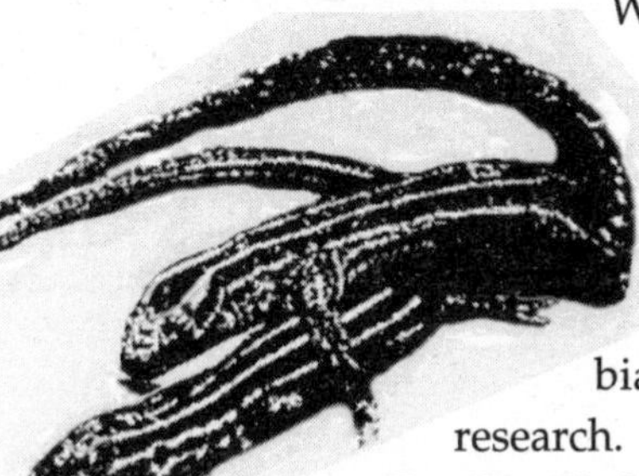

Dr. David Crews, a professor of zoology and psychology at the University of Texas who has been studying the whiptail lizard, observes that, "The species is a single clone." Not the Castro Street kind, of course. These Sisters are Doing It for Themselves. No sperm bank, no tiny lizard-sized turkey basters either: "The chromosomes of each lizard duplicate just before the ovum divides, producing genetically complete and genetically identical eggs."

Clever, eh? You might think this species presents a great opportunity to study sex among lesbian lizards. Or lesbian sex among lizards, however you wanted to approach the subject. Unfortunately, the scientists who were peeping at the glassed-in lizard lovemaking didn't quite see the project in either light. The word "lesbian" never even appears once in the report.

Instead, according to the article, these unisexual whiptail lizards go through "the motions of sex." Not sex, you understand, but the "motions of sex." How one can successfully separate sex from the motions of sex, I'm not really sure. In any case, what these horny little female lizards do in twosomes is, so the article describes it, to "engage in courtship displays and mounting behavior" during which "the male-like lizard curls over the other lizard and grasps her."

"Male-like" lizard. You see the conceptual problem here, I'm sure. One is male-like and the other is simply female, based on nothing but their relative positions and activity or passivity during sex. No legitimization of lesbianism at all, not even to distinguish the pair in lesbian terminology, as *Cnemidophorus uniparens butchus* and *Cnemidophorus uniparens femmis*.

It doesn't stop there. "The lizard that has just ovulated has a surge of progesterone, which causes her to act like a male, and then after a week or so her ovaries become larger and secrete estrogen, and she reassumes the female's part."

Here's the poetry in motion: the "top" lizard (why not call her Butch) slips her tail under her partner. After the mounting and the passionate tail-curling and grasping and gasping, the lizards assume the characteristic copulatory "doughnut" position.

And away they go.

So—a female lizard who consensually jumps the bones of another female lizard is "acting like a male"? Note again the title of the piece, "Does pseudosex enhance virgin birth?" Here is photographic, visible evidence right in front of your eyes of two female lizards doing the wild thing with each other. Yet this is not considered sex but "pseudosex" to some psocalled "objective" pscientists. And since there aren't any males in the species at all, these lady lizards can fuck each other's reptilian brains out but they're still all considered *virgins?* I'm psorry, but this psexist language and homophobic lesbian lizard invisibility verges on pseudoscience, if not plain old pstupidity.

Of course I have my own cultural biases. I see these little lesbian lizards as a sterling model of political correctness: every ten to fourteen days, the scientists note, the two female lizards switch roles. Yes. They *switch roles*. Imagine such a thing! Egalitarian sexual relationships even in the sandy desert among our reptile sisters! The whip-tail wraparound motion might be just a little kinky, but if your body came equipped with a long, supple, tapered tail, surely in the throes of passion you'd at least want to employ it to entwine, wouldn't you?

Scientists have, so far, only been able to observe this so-called "male-like" mounting of "the female" in the confines of captivity. And thus, the article says, their behavior poses a riddle for the befuddled researchers: if these "motions of sex" go on in the wild as well as in the lab, the professors are left wondering, "What reproductive purpose does it serve?"

It's true that some animal behaviors in captivity are less frequent or absent in an animal's natural environment. But if one is going to ask the *purpose* of one female lizard humping another female lizard, why limit your speculation to the wild? What *purpose* does it serve in the lab?

At first it was thought the "pseudosexual" behavior might be merely a "useless vestige of a former way of life." What an insulting way to look at lesbian sexuality.

But now, the researchers think that "perhaps the whiptail is more likely to ovulate when she's with a male-like female." They arrived at this hypothesis when it was found that "isolated females" (in other words, ones who don't engage in this "pseudo-sex") take longer to lay their eggs. "By going through this pseudo-sexual behavior," the whiptails "maximize the number of eggs they lay."

So here we have it, the ugly little core of moralistic, moronic anthropocentrism: if sex has a "purpose" for these lizards, the purpose *must* be procreation. They're all female, so all they must be interested in is eggs, eggs, and more eggs. Everything for the sake of the eggs.

As she's portrayed in *Discover*, the pathetic little lizard might as well be whining, wearing one of those tiny Disney-mouse babushkas: "Oh pity me, I can't help it, I'm just struggling to do what's best for my dear little ones..." or in the confessional: "Please, Father, forgive me, for I have sinned: I'm forced to pretend to be male for the sake of my family, oh dear oh dear. But at least

I'm still a *virgin...*"

"Parthenogenesis has its advantages," the professor admits, and he'll get no argument from me on that score. But he goes on to say that "the most obvious" advantage is "higher potential population growth, since all of these lizards (rather than half) can produce eggs."

Can you believe these scientists?! Here we have a species of lesbian lizards willing to performing interesting, even acrobatic lesbian sex acts in public, and not only don't these white coats have the guts to admit they are observing anything lesbian, they don't even seem to realize the significance of what it is they are studying: a species of lesbian animals having fun. Fun fun fun having sex. "There may be a point to it but what could it be?" Duh.

They can't even bring themselves to acknowledge that since the species is all female, when they mate with each other their sexual behavior is lesbian *by definition*.

If this article represents the progress in scientific thinking about sexuality in the ivy-covered halls of knowledge even on such a lowly level as a lezzie *lizard*, is it any wonder we human dykes are still considered second-class queers by the world at large?

In stark contrast to the puzzled lizard-watchers is an article from the October 1992 issue of the *Journal of NIH Research*. This piece pulls no punches. It's a description of a study of gay male flies—the insect, not the trousers, kind—called "The Genetics of Homosexuality." Well, good. Tell it like it is.

But here we lesbians encounter a different kind of invisibility. Again, lesbianism is nowhere mentioned—we're just lumped in with the guys. It would be more accurate to call this report "The Genetics of Male Homosexuality." Even among the *arthropoda* and the *squamata*, we lesbians seem to be caught between a rock and a hard place: distorted or forgotten.

But maybe that's not so bad in some cases. So far, the report comments, "no one has found a good rodent model of genetically based homosexuality." I'll be just as glad if it turns out there are no lesbian rats.

This article presents a study done at the National Cancer Institute of a "neglected" genetic variant of *drosophila melanogaster*—commonly known as the fruit fly. Discovered in 1963, the male genetic variant fly shows behaviors that the researchers describe as "somewhat comparable to homosexuality."

This type of genetic strain is called the "fruitless" variety. They don't say why, though I suppose it's because they don't have any offspring. I think it rather oxymoronic to be called a fruitless fruit fly. But these fellas do okay for themselves. In contrast to the theories about the lesbian lizards, reproduction is not considered to be uppermost in their tiny minds. Oh no—these are supersexed flies. All members of the fruitless variety are genetic males. And, we are told, "The fruitless males are attracted to wild-type males, other fruitless males, and females."

In other words, these guys will go for anything that drones.

"But when attracted to another fly, the fruitless males engage in a type of courtship behavior that is rare in wild-type males: they scurry around to the back of the appealing fly and lick its genitals."

Notice that the behavior of these fruitless flies is never labeled "pseudosex" or described as assuming "female-like" behavior.

"When groups of fruitless males are put together, they line up, mouthparts-to-tail-to-mouthparts, forming long courtship chains with each fly courting the fly in front and being courted by another from behind."

The article continues: "Although the flies' sex organs and sperm are fully functional, males that are homozygous for the fruitless trait do not mount and inseminate females; they are behaviorally infertile. In addition, wild type and other fruitless males, for some as yet unexplained reason, are sexually attracted to fruitless males."

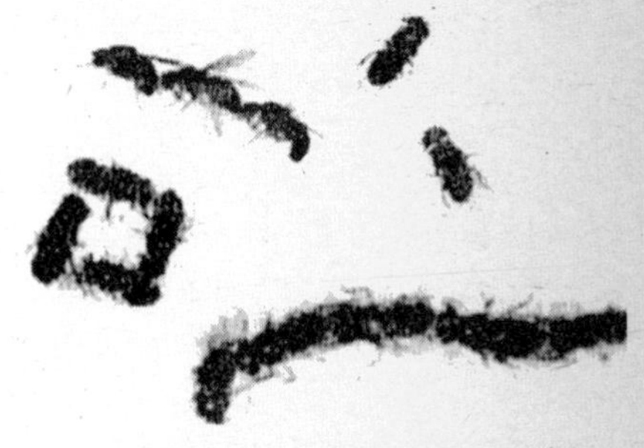

So fruitless males attract each other. It's no wonder, since they are homozygous. And they also attract the swinging wild type male flies—the genderbenders.

Wild thang, you make my feelers twang. You can see the undercurrent of orgiastic abandon, of unbridled homoerotic male sexuality as these flies zip around the petrie dish in ever-changing daisies and lengthening combinations.

This journal article has a very different tone from the lizard study. You get the feeling from the language of the report that the insects are attractive, everybody likes them, and that they are out there having a really hot time. Dancing the night away—the samba, line dancing, whatever. Clicking tiny castanets, shaking marimbas. The laboratory studying these bugs is a-buzz with enthusiasm.

I don't think this is a coincidence. Scientists are people—and all ideas about the animals and phenomena scientists study are colored by the cultural assumptions they bring with them.

In my view, the whiptail lizard has yet to have her lesbian reality validated. Rather than holding her head up proud, she has to go around dragging her tail, because it's such a drag to be a lizard in drag.

Whereas the scientists studying the fruitless fly say they are now busy trying to "clone the genes responsible for the fruitless phenotype." They want more of 'em! "The work might someday contribute to the development of genetically-engineered sterility useful in pest control," they say optimistically.

Less flies, more fun for each fly.

It's not as if these fruitless flies aren't put down at all. The article is, overall, very upbeat, but there are some subtle signs of disparagement. For one thing, the flies are called "mutants," which isn't a very nice thing to say about anybody. They are also mentioned in the context of being "pests," another pejorative term. And even though they *could* reproduce if they wanted to, the status of these flies is covertly diminished by the label "fruitless"—as if there's something "less" about them, that they are missing something.

And that's not right. For surely, if any *drosophila melanogaster* deserves to be called a *fruit* fly, it's these guys. And, though none of the scientists has noted it, the queer little fruitless fly has added a whole new facet to the term "buggery."

Click Click

Everybody says that the computer revolution is changing the way we communicate, and even the way we think. What has gone unrecognized so far is that the computer revolution is the greatest technological advance of all time for lesbian sexuality.

I'm not talking about access to the InterNet, the WorldWide Web. It's nice that people can connect and meet other lesbians and gay men and have bulletin board discussions and websites and so on, but that's just a drop in the bucket.

And forget the porno pictures and the virtual reality sex experiments. In fact I'm not talking about the content of anything you can gain access to or download on your computer at all.

I mean that we are on the verge of profound—even evolutionary—changes that directly promote lesbianism.

I was watching a TV show about computer literacy the other day, and the announcer said that most people unfamiliar with computers have to be trained in the simplest facets of computer operation. Some secretaries for large companies have even had trouble mastering the finger dexterity necessary to double-click on a mouse button.

Those secretaries who have trouble wiggling their fingers rapidly and subtly enough to perform mouse button double-clicking are not likely to be lesbians.

Right now, the most basic, essential high-tech skill that everyone needs to acquire to even begin to utilize the computer as a tool is: a finger dexterity that approaches the lesbian level.

Lesbian computer personnel already know very well how to double-click, triple-click, multiple-click and even perform stunts like the loop-the-loop on their mouses, since they do them all the time on their spouses.

Lesbians are already expertly-skilled, familiar with the most delicate moves necessary to inspire what Gertrude Stein called the Tender Buttons, so mouse buttons are a snap. In fact, lesbians probably have the fastest, most adept, most well-developed, most sensitive, and best all-around mouse-button-pushing fingers in the history of human evolution.

Continuing to use a mouse gives lesbians even more finger-muscle-building exercise than a weekend with their honey at the Sybaris.

Mouse-button-clicking dexterity has some important benefits for straight women, too. It can help teach those straight women who are libidinally-challenged how to masturbate. They can use this practical skill in tandem with those sexual-awareness self-help groups that show straight women how to find their own vaginas. Just move your hand up a little higher, dear, and pretend you're zipping around your mousepad.

And, too, it forces straight men to practice, all day long, the subtle finger motion necessary for adequate heterosexual foreplay and satisfaction of their female partners.

And trackballs? Even better. Slide your finger around on one of those for awhile if you've never done it before, and see what I mean.

And the newest technology, the accupoint device used on laptops and notebook computers, has the most subtle action of all. The slightest motion produces an immediate on-screen reaction, and it has a rubbery feel to it. For greatest finger dexterity practice, you can even alternate: use the accupoint when you have the laptop away from your desk, and the mouse or trackball when you've hooked the laptop to a computer docking station.

We don't have to "recruit" women to become lesbians—women become lesbians-in-training today simply by working in modern offices.

If rightwing engineers ever realize what they've inadvertently done to promote the sexual activity of the average lesbian, they'll be so angry they'll want to cursor. And then they'll be scrambling to replace lesbian-friendly computer pointing devices with some kind of a fat tubular thing that attaches to the side of the computer that you'd have to grab onto and rub up and down, and with a trigger-like handle instead of a button.

Oh wait, they've already done that. It's called a joystick. But they're popular on video games, not computers. They're much more cumbersome and less portable than the nice little compact button devices—so I guess we're safe for the foreseeable future.

The opposable thumb developed so early humans could grasp tree-branches and hold simple objects. As they got better at holding things, they learned to make tools, and that in turn reinforced the dexterity of the thumb.

So the more we practice mouse-clicking, track-ball swirling, and accupoint nudging, the stronger our forefingers are likely to become.

And according to the theory of evolution, the more computers become integrated into human life, the more lesbians will find a favorable climate and proliferate, by a process of natural selection.

Who knows what kind of new, more sensitive yet more powerful finger skeletal and musculature structures will develop as a result of all this? And all to the betterment of lesbian eroticism!

Thanks to the computer revolution, today's lesbians are enhancing our sexual performance capabilities every time we plug our laptops into a computer dyking station.

Coming In Loud and Clear

The human ear picks up sound waves, the eye detects light waves. But our bodies are surrounded by other waves that we can't detect at all. X-rays, radio waves, TV waves, and microwaves are bouncing around all over the place. These waves require some kind of equipment in order for us to pick up the signals—like a television antenna or a satellite dish.

But nobody knows how many different kinds of waves we haven't even discovered yet are out there jumping around.

For some people, the concept that we are surrounded by invisible undulating waves that are real yet imperceptible is difficult to imagine. But in the gay and lesbian community, just about everybody is aware of a kind of invisible signal transmitted between us. It's a sort of radar that we call "gaydar." Right?

Well, what if gaydar isn't just a queer kind of intuition we have, but is actually similar to radar? Suppose the invisible waves we pick up on our gaydar are *real* waves just like radio waves or microwaves?

What if lesbians and gay men send and receive these waves—and often aren't even conscious of doing it—because we simply have the right equipment, like a kind of built-in satellite dish or ham radio, to pick each other up?

Now, I'm not talking about actual optic or acoustic data, like gestures or symbols or a Romanovsky and Phillips album. If you encounter a woman with a crewcut except for one long thin pigtail down her back, and she has a gleaming platinum labyris around her neck big enough to dice carrots, you don't have to be a rocket scientist to realize she's far into the ultra-violet end of the visible spectrum.

What I'm talking about is when someone is not obviously gay or lesbian—but *something* about them makes you know they must be. Sometimes these people are not even aware themselves that their transmitter is on and sending. Yet *you know*. The "vibes" are there. Your internal gaydar receiver is strong enough to detect their signal right through all the interference.

In fact, some gay men and lesbians are so good at bringing in signals that they are like walking giant radar receivers probing space. A few gay men are so fine-tuned they can probably pick up signals from a new moon circling Uranus. Some lesbian gaydar is so wide-ranging it can detect wave pulses throbbing across distant galaxies, and so strong it can pierce right through an aluminum-shielded crab salad nebula at a pot-luck luncheon.

Such people have very sophisticated gaydar equipment that they've probably maintained in peak condition—because to really pick up on some distant heavenly body, you have to have a top-notch satellite and keep up with the dish.

It may be that almost everyone has the capacity for gaydar, but in most people it remains underdeveloped. Certain things will facilitate transmission. When you come out to yourself, you've upgraded your technology to solid-state. And once you come out to people around you, your circuits can become fully integrated.

Some people who don't transmit any gaydar signals at all themselves might still be doing relay, bouncing the signals from one station to another. Like when your grandma introduces you to her friend's granddaughter, saying, "Something tells me you two have a lot in common..."

Or maybe this has happened to you: A lesbian friend calls you up to say she's met someone she really likes, but the woman is not a lesbian. Then your friend introduces you to this straight woman and you know, *you know*, this "straight woman" is just waiting for countdown transmission to get off the launchpad. Your friend can't believe it—her gaydar has been temporarily muted, but yours is functioning perfectly and can translate the profusion of incoming signals into useful information. Then a month later you get another phone call, from the two of them, long distance. From some lesbian guesthouse in Saugatuck where they are spending a romantic weekend. They are so amazed that they're in love! This kind of gaydar signal triangulation can occur in many configurations.

When your mind is in a particular state, your brain wave has a characteristic shape. Scientists have been mapping brain wave patterns for some years now. We know what the Alpha wave looks like, and the Theta wave, and Delta wave, and others. Eventually someone—probably some queer scientist—will be the first to identify and chart the profile of the Lambda wave.

Once the Lambda wave pattern has been mapped, it can be further analyzed and subdivided to distinguish pure G wave and L waves from the combined Lambda wave form, and maybe even the theoretical Q wave can finally be charted.

Waves have to travel through something—some medium. Like air or water. And that will affect the wave's speed. Lambda waves are undoubtedly boosted in locations with more favorable atmospheric conditions. Like the sea breezes of Provincetown. While in a place like Selma, Alabama, where the air might be a bit thicker, the Lambda wave signals might encounter a great deal of resistance, and would therefore be more intermittent.

Atmospheric pockets that help gaydar waves move faster tend to form in large urban centers, but Lambda wave activity can be found almost anywhere, if one has the right equipment to detect them. People in really isolated places might need to rely on some kind of echo-location to get their gaydar functioning properly.

Waves are also affected by what they encounter in their path, and this is called "interference." Constructive interference from other waves can actually strengthen a wave form when the two waves travel in tandem. Constructive interference of Lambda waves undoubtedly occurs when the straight mayor of a large city marches in a gay pride parade. Destructive interference, on the other hand, fights against the wave pattern and can dissipate it, jamming signals. For example, when someone like Pat Buchanan broadcasts his hate messages, White noise jams up the air waves for everybody else.

Waves don't just travel through space, of course; they also travel through time. If the amplitude gets large enough, and the speed of the waves increase, their cumulative effects might reach perceptible levels. For example, some people think that highly visible straight men are responsible for the increase in lesbian awareness that we've witnessed recently, like Howard Stern, who brought two straight women in bikinis with him on the *Tonight Show* to kiss each other on television. But my guess is that the large lesbian wave we are on now is the cumulative effect, over a long period of time, of some invisible but very fast, rapidly increasing undulations coming from lesbian bodies worldwide.

People who meditate can consciously affect their brain waves. If both the sender and the receiver are aware that they are sending out L waves, the pulses of the waves might increase even to the point where the two transmitters decide to move into closer range, like mobile radar units moving nearer each other to amplify the signals to their maximum level by pulsating together.

If we can get the discipline of Lesbian and Gay physical sciences off the ground, Gay and Lesbian Studies will gain in status at academic institutions. If physics professors began working on research in Lambda wave theory, we would make inroads into the "hard" sciences like physics, math, and chemistry, as well as the soft, squishy social sciences and humanities. Maybe then university engineering departments could develop some defensive weaponry against incoming Hate waves. That would be a practical result of physics that would, for a change, directly benefit everyone.

With proper funding, perhaps science can eventually find an answer to the basic question: Where exactly do gaydar waves originate, and where are the signals received? We know that people's bodies are like big electromagnets, and our brains transmit electromagnetic waves all the time, just like a TV tower. But the exact location of gaydar is a highly convoluted subject. Neurologists have wrinkled their furrows over the matter, but it's still a grey area.

The so-called "gay-brain" neurons of the interstitial nuclei of the anterior hypothalamus regions 2 and 3 would be the likeliest spot to poke around with electrodes for electrical activity. But would you be nervy enough to volunteer as a subject? Since it's a risky business, you'd want assurances that the surgeon who was sawing into your head was absolutely even-handed, and that the person who was conducting the research was not someone who had an ax to grind.

Very likely, it will be a long time before any research on gays and lesbians is truly and completely non-invasive. So until then, whether or not we can safely submit ourselves to scientific study is, as far as I'm concerned, a no-gay-brainer.

Coupledom and Dumber

I'll be at a lesbian concert enjoying the show, and then, in the middle of her set, the performer onstage will say:

"Any couples here celebrating their tenth anniversary?"

One or two joined-at-the-hip lesbian couples in the audience will jump up and wave their four hands together in the air like some upended quadrupeds.

And we're all supposed to clap.

Even though maybe just yesterday one of these women confided to me that her long-term relationship feels "suffocating."

"Great!" gushes the performer. "How 'bout fifteenth?"

A few more women who are very likely bored to death with each other, or terminally codependent, or both, raise their hands.

"Twentieth?! Yeah! Way to go! Congratulations!"

And the rest of us again are obliged to applaud and smile and cluck our congratulations.

Why? Why is this the way to go? Go where?

Here we are, free women, no longer saddled with heterosexual mating practices, but we fall right into them anyway!

Oh, I know we're supposed to be supportive of lesbian coupledom since, the reasoning goes, society does not encourage lesbian relationships. But who encourages long-term unhappily-coupled lesbians to part, for heaven's sake—unless it's the next lover of one of them who is waiting patiently in the wings?

I admit that people do have a tendency to pair up. I've tended in that direction myself. And I realize that this tendency might not be an insidious invention of heterosexuals. Nevertheless, contrary to prevailing assumptions, "coupledom" is not a saintly state to which all lesbians and gay men—or even all straight people—aspire. Coupledom just as often as not leads to "couple-itis," a terrible chronic sickness that leaves its victims mentally and emotionally impaired.

Lesbian couples are always in danger of falling victim to couple-itis. I'm not sure why this is, unless it's the intense pressure some dykes feel to assure their straight relatives and friends that lesbianism can be just as nonthreatening—i.e. dull—as heterosexuality.

Whatever its etiology, couple-itis can change two very interesting self-motivated women into one boring partnership in paralysis.

Couple-itis is rarely fatal (except to friendships) but is definitely debilitating in its later, frightening stages, when two separately articulated lives can pathologically fuse together like some degenerative joint disease.

Firmly-coupled women may not even be aware they've contracted couple-itis. If a couple always socializes with the also-coupled, this reinforces symptoms at the same time it masks them from detection.

Here's how you can tell if you have a problem. You long-time coupled-up lesbians, examine the conversations you engage in with your friends. Are you talking about politics, art, ideas? Or are you bitching about whose turn it is to mow the lawn?

You know what? Nobody else gives a damn which one of you mows the lawn. Aside from your immediate neighbors, most people won't care if you never mow your friggin lawn!

Lesbians suffering from couple-itis don't seem to realize this—an indication of their growing delusion that the entire world revolves around the constricting focus of their little relationship.

And surprise—nobody cares which of you is the better driver, either. Or which one of you forgot to take out the garbage last Tuesday. And nobody really cares which one of you was too tired, drunk, or bored to have sex with the other one.

Though that's a bit more interesting than the state of your lawn.

In the beginning of a lesbian relationship, a woman will often suddenly disappear off the face of the earth. Her friends will notice that she is missing. Has she died, or has she simply found a new girlfriend and fallen into a deep pit located somewhere in the vicinity of her bedspread?

This phenomenon is not necessarily symptomatic of couple-itis. But the resting phase after the first long sexual frenzy is a critical juncture: you can bounce back from the tendency to merge, and maintain a healthy relationship as two independent individuals—even if you move in together—or you can sink into the Melding Phase.

The Melding Phase is the first danger sign, the first serious indication of couple-itis. It is during the Melding Phase that identities begin to get blurred. For example, in *Lesbian Connection*, just last month, several letters that say "I" all the way through are *signed by two women!* This is definitely symptomatic of Melding.

As the condition worsens, lesbians in a couple stop using the word "I" altogether. This is the well-known "On-We" Symptom. Here ennui has set in, especially among friends who have to listen to each woman in the couple substitute "we" for "I" in even the most improbable situations.

Sometimes the coupled will even begin to speak to each other as if they have only one body: "I guess we never should have let that dentist talk us into doing that root canal, should we?" Or one of them will begin to assume the role of spokesperson, always saying "We," while her partner will almost stop speaking at all.

Friends of the afflicted will know the problem has accelerated when they try to arrange to do something with one of the women in the couple and are told, "Sure. I'd love to. Of course I'll have to ask (fill in name of partner) if it's okay..."

This is the Fusion Phase. The woman in the couple will consider this to be a matter of simple common consideration toward her partner. But to the friend, it may well sound as if she's saying, "Sure. I'd love to. Of course I'll have to ask mommy if it's okay for me to come out and play..."

Similarly, the coupled person will begin to assume any event she is invited to automatically means her lover is also invited, as if they were Siamese twins. She may ask, just as a courtesy, "You don't mind if (name of partner) comes along, do you?" But see how pale and peaked she becomes if the friend says, "Well, actually, I'd like to see just you for a change." Though the coupled person doesn't want to admit it to herself, she has come to feel strangely insecure about going to any social event without her partner. Pathological fusion has set in.

The worst stage of the syndrome, Acute Duopathy, is characterized by a weakening of the faculties, affecting mental acuity sometimes to the point of infantilism. It's a pitiful thing to watch a strong-willed dyke, who has demonstrated publicly for gay rights like a valiant warrior, turn to her lover and say in a coy, quavering puppy voice, "Hunn-neeey, would it be okay if we stopped off at the Wawly-mart on the way home? Pwease? I weally need some aspiwin..."

At this advanced stage of couple-itis, coupledom has turned this otherwise intelligent woman into a coupledummy.

Is there anything you can do in the fight against chronic couple-itis? Like bronchitis or sinusitis, couple-itis usually requires treatment to effect a reversal.

Some have attempted the drastic step of seducing one of the women afflicted. Some have even seduced both women in question, either separately or together. This emergency intervention is not usually advisable, because it can have the opposite effect from that intended. After the dust settles, the couple could become even more firmly fused and twisted together.

A less radical and probably more beneficial therapy involves changing social rituals around "breaking up." For instance, lesbians can begin celebrating when couples part in exactly the same way we celebrate the anniversary of when they got together. If you really want to go all out, you can throw the newly-ex-coupled the kind of big, joyous party you'd throw for Siamese twins who have just been successfully separated. Both women should be invited to the party as the guests of honor.

Celebrating may seem a strange, inappropriate or even tactless thing to do at such a time. It may even prove difficult logistically, if the two women refuse to be in the same room with each other. But eventually, throwing happy relationship-ending gatherings will be seen as gay events, events that counter the almost universal assumption that when a relationship ends, it's been a "failure." Maybe it's not a failure but a success, and it's ending because it's exactly the proper time for both women to move on—like a graduation ceremony marks the end of a stage in a person's education with a sense of accomplishment. You're finished with that relationship? Cheers! Yay! Mazeltov! How exciting! Congratulations! Way to go!

Lesbian performers can do their part to help, too. After prompting everyone in an audience to applaud for the long-time couples, they can ask from the stage, "And how many women here tonight are still close friends with every lover you've broken up with in the last ten years?"

I'll gladly applaud and heartily cheer for every lesbian who can stand up and claim that achievement.

Experimental Dykology

"To give voice to their aspirations and needs, visibly committed homosexuals of both sexes have formed national organizations. They attempt to improve the public image of homosexuals, to protect them from persecution and discrimination, and to give them a sense of personal dignity; but they are not oriented toward helping their members change their pathological sexual pattern."

You might think that quote comes from some right-wing hate literature. In fact, I read it in the *Comprehensive Textbook of Psychiatry,* a textbook for medical students published in 1967.

I can't even begin to cite all the socially-embedded prejudices that are discussed in this book under the guise of objectivity and scientific authority. But the above quote illustrates how actually political rather than scientific these pronouncements were. The "Sexual Deviations" chapter reads like a minefield; behind every clinical "diagnosis" and "treatment" one senses the untold damage done to countless gay, lesbian, and bisexual people by medical "experts" on the subject of sexuality who parroted, bolstered, and institutionalized the social intolerance of their day.

And they thought they were being compassionate and enlightened.

For example, they advise parents of any child who exhibits the slightest hint of homosexuality to grab the kid and run for the nearest psychiatrist's office, to get that kid some "treatment" before it's too late. I have several personal friends who were taken to be shrunk at the age of twelve or thirteen, when they developed an innocent crush on a schoolmate of the same sex. Their parents may even have gotten that advice from doctors who had read the *Comprehensive Textbook of Psychology.*

Back in the Sixties, my own parents were completely hostile to all mental health professionals. They firmly believed all psychiatrists were quacks, "headshrinkers," who either bilked people out of their money by charging outrageous fees for simply listening to their problems and then offering nonsensical Oedipal theories, or who sadistically and capriciously experimented on human brains through electroshock "therapy" and lobotomy. One of my mother's school classmates was locked up for years at Creedmore, and she blamed it all on the doctors.

Reading this psychiatry textbook, I can appreciate my parents' fears about the misuse of power by "shrinks"—first by getting labeled "aberrant," "deviant," "pathological," and then ground like pulp into their system and its "treatments."

"Once those guys get a hold of you they'll drive you crazy for sure," my mother said.

In 1973 the American Psychiatric Association eliminated homosexuality as a disease category. Bravo! We are no longer "pathological." And that's all well and good. But as far as I'm concerned, it's not enough that homosexuality has been dropped from the list of psychological disorders. Why hasn't homophobia been added to that list?

I know that some people dislike the term "homophobia" because, they argue, it makes hatred against gay people appear to be a psychological condition rather than a form of prejudice. They prefer to use the term "heterosexism."

Personally, it seems to me that the relationship between fear and hate is a complex one, and though the term heterosexism is sometimes more appropriate, homophobia is a useful word as well.

What are people afraid of today? Losing their jobs, going bankrupt, falling ill, not being able to take care of their families. Nuclear disaster, terrorism, gang violence, assault. Forest fires, earthquakes, flooding. With all the serious calamities that can befall, anxiety over something like sexual diversity sure looks like a genuine *phobia*. A "pathological pattern."

So when will modern-day psychiatrists and psychologists begin carefully examining the problem of homophobia *as a phobia*?

I mean, what is the big deal about two women going to bed together, for heaven's sake? As much as I like to think that lesbians are brilliant, creative, unique, and fascinating, and as much as I agree with Rita Mae Brown's heroine, Molly Bolt, in *Rubyfruit Jungle* that the difference between sex with men and sex with women is the difference between "a pair of roller skates and a Ferrari," I must also admit that the physical acts that lesbians and gay men do in bed *per se* are not all that different from the things that straight people do. In fact, many of the things I might do in bed with a woman lover could look, to a bystander, exactly like things that millions of straight men might do in bed with a woman lover.

The only difference is, we lesbians might do it better.

And that's one thing some straight male homophobes may be afraid of.

With all the psychological testing that has been developed and refined in our modern times, surely shrinks could come up with a barrage of "indicators" to test people's level of homophobia and where exactly it comes from. We need to devise a measure of how much fear is involved, and diagnostic tools for determining its source. Is it a distinct problem, or connected to irrational fear of diversity in general? Only then can therapies be developed—a first step toward curing the disorder.

Now, I'm not a psychiatrist or psychologist or therapist, but I'm going to offer a few preliminary suggestions for this kind of testing, just from a layperson's perspective, to light a fire under the butts of the professionals. I have formulated a series of questions to determine how deep the phobia goes. As my Uncle Henry the prison guard used to say, "It's a thankless job, but somebody's got to do it."

I've taken my cue from the Minnesota Multiphasic Personality Inventory (MMPI). To help psychology professionals evaluate and assess any straight woman client's level of lesbophobia, I have devised the Chicago Lesbophobic Indicator Test (CLIT). The following is a sample of test questions from CLIT:

Here are several pairs of activities or situations: show which one of each pair you like better.

1.) Would you rather march through
(A.) San Francisco in midsummer as part of a gay pride parade
(B.) Russia in midwinter as part of Napoleon's army

2.) Would you rather
(A.) be buried in the desert naked at noontime up to your neck in sand, next to a red ant colony
(B.) be tucked under a soft warm down comforter naked in bed at a ski lodge in the mountains, next to a lesbian

3.) Would you rather
(A.) be torn apart by hungry alligators
(B.) share a vegetarian lasagna with k.d. lang

4.) Would you rather be questioned by
(A.) a Mafia kingpin
(B.) a lesbian police officer

5.) Would you rather stand in line at the post office in front of
(A.) a lesbian mom
(B.) a gun-toting disgruntled ex-postal worker

6.) Would you rather
(A.) get a scalp massage from a woman with strong, supple fingers
(B.) get a migraine headache from a toxic airborne event

7.) Would you rather be intimate with
(A.) Emma Thompson
(B.) Hunter Thompson

8.) Would you rather have
(A.) a woman's hand cascading over your body
(B.) a mudslide cascading over your house

9.) Would you rather be the daughter of two members of
(A.) a lesbian activist group that is seeking a human rights ordinance
(B.) a satanic cult group that is seeking a human sacrifice

10.) Would you rather be rolling down the highway of love in
(A.) a pair of roller skates
(B.) a Ferrari

At this stage, the CLIT is still a fairly rough inventory. But even at this basic level, answers to questions like those above will determine if your female client is lesbophobic, and to what extent.

As we refine the CLIT's sensitivity, similar tests can also be developed for lesbophobic straight men, and for gaymalephobic straight women and straight men, biphobic, transphobic, etc. etc.

If you are a graduate student in psychology, you might want to show the CLIT to your straight female neighbors and ask them to look it over and take it, and make your evaluation a course project. Or you could make up your own list of questions and do the same. Let me know if you obtain any interesting results, as the CLIT is still very open-ended and has the potential for many adjustments, manipulations, and fine-tunings.

Once we have localized the parameters of homophobia as a *phobia*, the legions of therapists around today won't have to spend so much of their time patching us up and healing us from all the injuries we've sustained as the targets of misplaced hostility. Instead, they can spend more time treating the hostile and the homophobic—the people who have the real problem, and who may not even know how sick they are.

LOUISVILLE
Evansville
Terre Haute
INDIANAPOLIS
INDIANA
Champaign
DYKE VICTORY!

...The woman-loving women
in America were called dykes
and some liked it
and some did not.
They made love to each other
the best they knew how
and for the best reasons...

—Judy Grahn, from the poem
"A History of Lesbianism"
From *The Woman Whose Head Is On Fire,*
Crown Publishers

On The Road

With apologies to Jack Kerouac and Allen Ginsberg

In the month of July I was ready to head South. My girl and I had split up, and I wanted to take off. Deena Moriarty had fevered my brain with wild outlaw tales about the pow flash of that mad new generation of crazy wild hip festival dykes just a highway adventure down the road, and soon the whole gang would be headed for Cloudland.

She spun visions of the butch angels staggering out of the bohemian grottos of Frisco and the bop joints of Kansas City and the purple Village bar scene. The wild mad genius womyn writers scribbling their holy mantras on the satin lavender sky. The beatific earth mammas with their holy femme beads and chanting wails. All drunk with the crazy mad swirl of dykelove, looking for the pearl, the elusive pearl.

Out of the raving closets of despair they came, zooming the highways of america toward the new lesbian mecca, the sapphic vision of a swirling, mystical, mad communication nirvana happening in destinations with soulful names that sang up from my tongue like dharma prayers saying Hart, Bloomington, and Cloudland Cloudland Cloudland.

Deena Moriarty was at that time still a perky young lesbian with red tinted hair and a pierced lip. She and the other hip dykes were gearing up for the trip. Big Edna Kunkel had just driven in madly nonstop from Frisco with her swinging longhaired girl Tammy Snark. Since Big Edna had done the Cloudland gig before, she would drive the lead van with Tammy. Me—Sally Paradise—I could hop a ride with them. Carla Marx, the nutty surrealist tai chi angel poet, would ride along with us, too. In the other van Old Bell Lee would drive, along with Deena, and Old Bell's girl Alma Hassel, who was famous for her cool hip sneer. At that time I hadn't ever met Old Bell, but she was already a legend among our friends.

We knew it was risky, tumbling headlong down route 65 gambling our souls on a joyride into the dream world of lesbian nation. The mad holy visions of mindblasting prophecies of night fearlessly stripping away the barbwire chain fallen screen of dismal boytime reality. And memories of past festivals reminding us you have to decompress and decompress after you woefully leave a festival, too, because jump back into the womanlost world of malejive monotonous misery too fast and you get a painful case of the bends.

I got to Remi Boncoeur's house, where we were all supposed to meet, exactly on time. Big Edna's van wasn't there, and I was worried that they'd left without me. Then Deena Moriarty strolled out of the screen door and in her easy drawl told me that Big Edna and Carla Marx had gone off to get some grub for the road. Already we were freestyling on mad mystical dyketime!

Old Bell Lee and Alma Hassel, parked nearby, sat in their van making out for close to an hour till Big Edna and Carla came roaring back with a big bag of nourishing submarine sandwiches. Tammy showed up wearing her hip sneer but hadn't had a shower yet, and went into Remi's place to take one. Deena the outlaw lovechild of a forgotten back street joybinge and I caught up on old times on Remy's front steps. When we finally did get on the road that balmy duskfalling summer evening it was after dark but we were wired, knowing that we would be driving to the center of where everything converged with a bunch of wailing wild lesbians.

I've travelled the festival roads before with Big Edna and Tammy. Once I thought we wouldn't make it out of a truckstop alive when, at 6 a.m., we were the only women in the place, aside from two waitresses, and Big Edna and Tammy, those two mad crazy queers, spinning their wild visions of dykelove, were hanging all over each other, Tammy's long loose hair twining around Big Edna's flannel shirt buttons. I was glad we got out of there before we all got beat up or thrown in the slammer on some trumped up vagrancy charge.

Big Edna likes to read the roadmap while she drives seventy or eighty. She never figures out the right roads, just stares for minutes at a time blankly at the map while we careen like a magnet to our mystical destination. Just for kicks, sometimes she yells out the window, "I love women! I love all women!" Tammy usually keeps her eyes tight on the road so if Big Edna swerves too far while reading her roadmap she can reach out fast enough to snap back the wheel.

This trip, we were caravanning. That means the two vans stick together on the road. We keep in such a tight hip groove that whenever any one of us has to pee we signal so all seven of us can take that smooth crazyleaning turnoff at the next beatific rest stop on the windswept holy godforsaken flatlands of grunting rural Indiana.

And at every rest stop we hit on that naked laidout highway heading South, Carla Marx and Deena Moriarty made beelines for the pay phones to talk and talk while the rest of us, done peeing, stood around for twenty minutes eyeing the eerie fluorescent vending machines full of corn sweets and salty pretzels, and watched the sad arguing nuclear momendads in their big cars going nuts from the babycrying and kids all lollypop sticky cellophane.

Carla Marx had to keep calling Seattle to pick up a neverending intense marathon conversation about the universe and the true meaning of dykelove with this famous West Coast lesbian outlaw poet she was having a long distance intense affair with. Carla Marx even met the famous outlaw poet on the phone when the poet put an ad in the personals column of the gay newspaper and Carla, who gigged on classified ads at the time, took the call. It was a case of instant karma, right over the line. And cool Deena Moriarty kept calling her lover Vance, just cause she could never get enough of her sweet wailing jazzthroat talkrhythm.

Four rest stops later, around one in the blearyeyed morning, we found ourselves south of Indianapolis in the heart of Quayle Country. Big Edna was too tired to keep driving, so all seven of us had to stop at a mystical Motel 6 for the night. My head began to take a nosedive into my crazy nightmare vision of being lost on some endless stretch of road in some dreary flat republican vice president place like Indiana, dying feetstuck to the exitramp of terminal boredom.

But we got a snazzy double room at the old Motel 6 and I started feeling better, my bleak highway nightmare lifting. Big Edna and Tammy slept in one bed and Carla Marx and I in the other. Old Bell Lee and Alma Hassel somehow managed to wangle themselves a single room, with Deena Moriarty sleeping on their floor in a sleeping bag. They were supposed to get a 7 a.m. wakeup call and come knock on our door, but I woke up at 8 to find everyone still in bed except Big Edna, who was staggering around the room naked, barely awake.

Deena said she'd really like it if we could have a sit-down breakfast somewhere before we got going that morning, since it would be our last 'real meal' for the whole weekend. So Big Edna careened us over the highway to a little roadside diner that had a huge sign outside blinking neon Omelet House to treat ourselves to some savory midwestern coffeesteaming eggsizzling delicious food.

We walked in past a pack of men hanging outside, old men with army tattoos who stood staring at us blusterfaced. I felt very sorry for the matronly chick behind the counter, a holloweyed waitress battered bleak of brain so sad of soul under her beehive hairdo. It goes without saying the vibes were not good and then I got bummed because the decaf was Sanka in a packet. Tammy was bummed because they didn't make her staple road food, plain poached eggs on organic wheat toast, which they never make anywhere anyway. There was no non-smoking section, and Old Bell Lee got ticked about that, and then we all did, because everybody in the place smoked like a liverpool chimney. Carla Marx ordered some classic midwestern fresh homefries that turned out to be frozen potato shavings dumped in a greasy frying pan.

Near our beatvision formica table was a video game with some kind of Satanic picture on it, and a Six Million Dollar Man pinball machine with blinking dollar signs. The bad karma of the place began to well up till it was a physical pain and I thought I would freak but then I knew I'd only been zapped with a holy mystical menstrual cramp. I ducked into the bathroom with the little ladies' skirt icon on the door looking for the holy crazy tampax dispenser. I ducked my head back out to be sure it was the ladies' room, because hanging on the wall behind the toilet was no girlpadthing but a dull greymetal condom dispenser. It looked like it was probably manufactured in the fifties, and for two quarters it would slip you something called Hawaiian prophylactics. It had a picture on the front, of a tanned young barechested cat in jeans, and a young blonde bustychick wearing a lei was kneeling on the ground in front of him, rubbing her fluffyteasehead against his abdomen. Next to this machine was a contraption I'd never even seen before called a "Love Drops" dispenser with a picture of another blonde with her jungle red mouth pulled open as wide as chestskin during heart surgery, to catch this mouth rinse the machine would lay on you so that as the sign below the blonde said you would become "Irresistible."

The vision of this condom dispenser love drops mechanical karma in the ladies room so gassed me that my mind reeled. I knew immediately that I had stumbled upon the dull cranking metal heart of the heartland core of america's machine in a seedy toilet here in this crazy sleepy burg called Clarksville, Indiana.

I swooned with my revelation which reached an epiphany as I quickly crafted a mantric makeshift pad for my mystical sacred blood from a wad of old napkins in my jacket pocket. When I got back to the dyketable, Deena Moriarty was getting antsy because the old guys were leering so hard at her lip ring, and we decided to get back to the caravan.

We are still on this mystical holy road. Big Edna has gotten preoccupied with a facepimple and keeps staring in the swivel mirror above the dash. Tammy is absentmindedly fiddling with the radio and rooting around in the glovebox for chocolate. Carla Marx, sitting next to me behind them, is scribbling letters to her lesbian poet lover to keep up their mad neverending conversation during the times they can't be on the telephone. Every time we pass anything that reminds Carla of her wild Buddhist visions of the Chinese doctrine of dualism she quickly jots it down, like when we passed the "Moo and Oink" Restaurant and the "Tank and Tummy" Rest Stop.

As we make our way down the thick neck of the highway we find more rest stops and gas stops at hot bleak plastic southern gas station-convenience stores. I am feeling wired again because I have been to the very core of heterosex lovedrop hell and have emerged unscathed and now we are going to Cloudland on the velvet promise of girls, visions, and everything, and all across the country other hipdykes are taking to the road like us, aiming their sport utility vehicles toward that glistening lesbian mecca, each highway line a luminous spoke in the great cosmic mandala wheel down whose slender threads we are moving in the machinery of night. At its sacred hub I knew I'd find my safe haven, the euphoric new jazzed karmic cloudland dyke utopia of my wild crazy eternal longing, and there the pearl would be handed to me. We are waiting to cross the tracks of the endless boxcars boxcars boxcars and my head is bonging bonging bonging with our ecstatical rhythmical run-on adjectival adventure on the road.

Dragonflies Above Our Nation

"...And I dreamed I saw the bombers, riding shotgun in the skies, turning into butterflies above our nation... "

—Joni Mitchell, *Woodstock*

When seven thousand lesbians get together for an open-air celebration, it does seem like another world.

We often make jokes about the Michigan festival and other outdoor festivals held in some secluded woods as "Lesbian Woodstock" events. And it's certainly true that by and large, lesbians don't go to the festivals to hear specific performers any more than hippies went to Woodstock specifically to see Crosby, Stills, Nash and Young. They go primarily for the experience of being in a place where lesbians, if just for a brief time, are in the vast majority. And, of course, to meet other lesbians. The Michigan festival is open to all women, not just lesbians, but lesbians there are ten-to-one, not one in ten.

At the Michigan festival last year, I sat among 300 women in the audience at the Acoustic Stage, in the natural outdoor amphitheater formed by the gently dipping landscape. We were listening to pianist Liz Story.

Liz Story is, I believe—like Joni Mitchell and Bonnie Raitt—not a lesbian herself, but has a large following among lesbians. She was onstage performing some of her beautiful solo piano compositions.

"As a musician, I notice all kinds of sounds," she said, introducing her next song. "And I've discovered that electric devices tend to hum in the key of A. On the other hand, insects tend to buzz in the key of F."

So, she said, she had composed a piano piece in the key of F that she calls "Things with Wings."

And she started playing it.

She was not many bars into the music—which had lots of reverberating bass notes—when someone in the crowd raised an arm and pointed straight upward. Many of us looked up toward the sky to see what she was pointing to.

There were dragonflies—first dozens, then *hundreds of them*—flying in the air above the audience. The dragonflies seemed to be swooping and dipping and gliding along to the music.

Liz Story kept on playing. A murmur went through the crowd as more women became aware of the amazing sight of all these dancing dragonflies. It was a spectacular, magical moment. Not only did the dragonflies seem to be drawn directly by the music, but they looked happy, gay, exuberant as they danced and dipped in the air.

It wasn't Woodstock. And we weren't hallucinating.

But honest to goddess, there they were—and suddenly these dragonflies looked to me like they could be little living labyrises, fluttering joyfully above us.

Our modern labyris lesbian symbol, often thought of as a double-sided Viking ax, is actually thought to have originated much further back, in the ancient Minoan matriarchy on Crete—where you can still see labyrises painted on the walls of the palace at Knossos today. This labyris design was not a weapon, but a butterfly, symbolic of metamorphosis and transformation.

At extraordinary moments like the "Things With Wings" dragonfly dance at our "Lesbian Woodstock," it's not at all difficult to believe that there really is a continuity between ancient women's mysteries and modern women's dreams.

Highly Outspoken

The Stonewall Rebellion has finally merited mention in the venerable Encyclopaedia Britannica. So we can rest assured that the gay and lesbian rights movement is, at long last, up there on the map of significant world information.

"Homosexual rights movement" appears in volume 6 right after "homopteran," a type of bug that feeds on plant juices and includes "some 32,000 species of sucking insects."

I'm glad that now we are considered at least as important as sucking insects—though I know that some people still think we're no better than homopterans.

Here's part of what the encyclopaedia says about the "homosexual rights movement":

> The beginning of militant homosexual activism can virtually be dated. At about 3:00 AM on June 28, 1969, the Stonewall Inn, a homosexual bar at 53 Christopher Street in Greenwich Village, was raided by New York City police. Instead of passively accepting the situation (as in the past), the some 200 homosexuals present began taunting the police and throwing debris; the riot lasted 45 minutes and resumed on succeeding nights. Protest rallies ensued; homosexual rights organizations proliferated from the 1970s on. "Stonewall" or "Christopher Street" came to be commemorated annually in late June in Gay Pride Week (alternatively Gay and Lesbian Pride Week), not only in U.S. cities but in cities in several other countries. What Oscar Wilde had called the "love that dared not speak its name" had, by the late 20th century, become highly outspoken.

That last sentence seems like a bit of editorializing, when you consider all the places in the world we still can be imprisoned or killed for being Out—but the significance of the Stonewall rebellion is properly acknowledged.

As a matter of fact, "to stonewall" has been in use as a verb at least as far back as the days of Oscar Wilde himself. Meaning: "to engage in obstructive parliamentary debate or delaying tactics," "to be uncooperative, obstructive, or evasive," and "to refuse to comply or cooperate with."

Do you realize how incredibly fortunate we are that we just happened to get such an appropriate word as "Stonewall" associated with our civil rights movement?

In retrospect, everybody acknowledges that by the late Sixties, the situation of "homosexuals" had reached a social crisis; the harsh police repression and the growing notion of "gay power" were going to clash somewhere. Gay and lesbian bars were regularly raided. Bar patrons were fed up, and they weren't going to take it anymore.

Think about it. Of all the gay bars where a gay riot might have started, the spark ignited at a place called the Stonewall Inn.

Stonewall. Such a solid, movement kind of a name. It has a real ring to it. So American sounding, too—reminiscent of Stonewall Jackson the old warrior, the people's president. (Most people have forgotten the word's association with Republican evasiveness during the Watergate scandal.) And yet, even though it's so solid-sounding, "to stonewall" is also vague and gender-neutral.

Suppose the bar that the cops had arbitrarily chosen to raid that hot summer night after Judy Garland's funeral had been called, say, the Nutbush? Or the Dungeon?

"The Nutbush Revolution"? It would have been really hard to convince most lesbians to join forces with gay men for the "Nutbush Revolution." With a name like that, even groups like PFLAG might never have gotten off the ground.

"The Dungeon Revolution" would have had its own thorny problems.

"The St. Mark's Bathhouse Revolution"? Not many lesbians

could wrap themselves around that name either.

Eyewitnesses to the riots still aren't in agreement about whether it was a drag queen or a dyke who threw the first punch at one of the cops.

Whoever it was, by all accounts there were certainly some lesbians involved in the fray, though the Stonewall was predominantly a gay male drag bar. In fact, there was a lesbian bar in Greenwich Village at the time of the riots that was not far from the Stonewall Inn. When the rioting began, some women ran out from that bar to join the fighting on Christopher Street.

That place was called Kookies.

Good thing the cops hadn't raided Kookies that night, and the rioting hadn't erupted there. The "Kookies Revolution" would never have been taken seriously by anybody.

What's in a name? A lot, when it's the rallying cry of a social movement.

Yes, we were very lucky the police just happened to pick on the Stonewall that night.

Skating Down Memory Lane

When I was seventeen, one of my best childhood friends became the youngest professional team member in the history of the New York Roller Derby.

Lorie was a tough kid, all right, but also very sweet.

I never went to a single one of her games. That seems weird to me now. They showed the roller derby on TV, and sometimes I'd watch it on my parents' black-and-white set. I saw these muscular women speeding crazily around the rink in big clunky lace-up roller skates, bonking into each other as hard as they could to push each other off the track.

Not my thing.

At the time, Lorie and I had already drifted apart. We were still friends, but we didn't spend much time together anymore. Once we had both been wild about dancing to Brenda Lee and Roy Orbison and the Shirelles. But while she was developing her skill as a human flying battering ram, I was developing my hippie sensibilities, listening to Bob Dylan records, reading the *Village Voice* and singing "The Lion Sleeps Tonight" with the folkie crowd in Washington Square Park.

Lorie's professional name was Big Bertha. At seventeen, Big Bertha was already making quite a bit of money for a teenager, and had a lot of fans. When Lorie and I did manage to spend time together, I would proudly show her the latest guitar chords I had mastered. She would smile and proudly show me the wounds she'd acquired in the rink.

"And look at these blood blisters on my heels!" she'd say, pulling down her socks. I'd look, but with squinting eyes and a grimace on my face.

She also told me about some of her teammates. I even recall her using the words "butch" and "femme" when she talked about them, but I never asked her what that meant. I had just the vaguest sense that these roller derby queens were lesbians. Maybe that's why I never went to Lorie's games—scared I'd find out something about myself I didn't want to know.

Now I kick myself to think what an opportunity I missed. Imagine! Thirty years ago, my friend Lorie could have gotten me into the women's dressing room at the roller derby! I could have hung out there with her if I'd wanted! What unrecorded lesbian herstory must have been made in such a place! And my lesbian life might have begun far earlier than it eventually did.

You're probably thinking that Lorie was a dyke, but she wasn't. In one of those twists of fate, the hippie was the one who eventually got all dyked out, and the youngest roller derby star got married to Joe, a very nice fellow who, I believe, worked as a hairdresser.

Not gay. Neither one of them.

I went to their wedding. I think I only saw her three or four times after she got married, and that was very long ago.

Lorie and Joe have been married now for twenty five years. They live on Long Island, not too far from my mother, and when they heard I was in town, they arranged to come get me and take me to their house for a visit.

When you meet old friends again that you haven't seen in years, you wonder how they are going to react when they find out that you're gay. Knowing Lorie's history, I figured that at least she wasn't likely to be homophobic.

I came out to Lorie right away, in the car, and as I'd thought, it was fine. But of course I was very curious about her roller derby years.

"Well," she said, "I was always straight. Some of the women would come on to me, but they were very, oh, I don't know—gallant, sort of. They never tried to force themselves on me in any way."

"How many of the women in the roller derby back then were lesbians?"

"Oh, most of them were gay. Not just the women, either," she said. "The male roller derby stars were mostly gay, too."

"Really? I didn't know that. Were they very butch and femme?"

"Oh, yeah," she said as we pulled into her driveway. "There was a lot of butch-femme stuff among all lesbians in those days, not just the roller derby."

"So I've heard," I said, tickled that she knew something of lesbian history.

"But then that was out for a long time. Lately it's been coming back again, though," she said.

"Yeah, I've heard that too," I said, smiling.

"You remember my wedding? My maid of honor was a lesbian. Still is. She and her lover live in Valley Stream. So I hear about what's going on."

What a pleasant surprise this visit was turning out to be.

Lorie and Joe have no children, but they've made it their cause to help animals. They take in strays. They had about thirty dogs and cats—including dogs with three legs, and cats with leukemia and heart trouble—at their house, and I was introduced to all of them.

Joe was very genial and friendly. He's been a tradesman for many years now. "I gotta admit to you," he said, pouring me a cup of tea, "I had a little problem with the lesbians at the roller derby. I felt a little threatened by those women Lorie hung around with in those days. I mean, I could see a few of them wanted to date her. Like that Gabby Grazziano—remember, Lorie?"

"Gabby Grazziano, yeah," Lorie said, smiling.

"Who?"

"She was in the roller derby, too. Back before Lorie and I got married, when we were engaged, Lorie went to California for a roller derby series. And when she was coming home, I went to La Guardia airport to pick her up. And there was Gabby Grazziano, already there, waiting for the plane, with this big bouquet of beautiful red roses for Lorie."

He said this all in a very good-natured tone of voice, like it was a pleasant memory for him, too.

Joe said that as soon as he saw Gabby, he got angry, jealous that she was bringing flowers for his fiancee. In that wonderful New York accent I miss so much since I've moved to the Midwest, he told me, "I mean, she knew we were engaged. So I sez to Gabby, 'Hey, I thought the fee-*ann*-see was s'posed ta bring the flowers.' "

Gabby, Joe said, threw her head back and gave him a tough-girl look and said, "Hey, well, Mister Fee-*ann*-see, I don't see *you* wit no flowers."

And Joe had to admit that she was right—it hadn't even occurred to him.

"I was on my toes after that," he said jovially, "'cause I knew I'd better show Lorie how nice I could be, with that kind of competition."

You know, I thought to myself, that's the kind of situation you might see today on a progressive TV sitcom like *Roseanne*. But this happened in real life almost thirty years ago—years before I even came out to myself.

Sometimes I forget that even though our society is riddled with homophobia, there have always been many straight people like Lorie and Joe, who really are our allies, who are interested in our culture, and who can laugh with us rather than against us.

"Well," Joe said shyly, "I could afford to be generous about it afterwards, because I was the one who got the girl."

Auld lang Sign

The turning of the year is a time to reflect on the past and plan for the future. I was thinking how incredible it seems today that not very many years ago we would speculate, over at the *Outlines* newspaper office, whether k.d. lang was a lesbian or not. Imagine that?

"She's *got* to be," we'd all agree. She had all the vibes. That special lang twang thang triggered our gaydar like a fire alarm. But at the time, she was just one of a number of singers, actresses, and other public figures who we were sure must be gay, but who weren't saying, and who weren't giving any interviews to the gay press.

When the film *Salmonberries* came out, the speculation was over, in my opinion, since she came Out cinematically for all the world to see. Nobody—well, okay, no *gay person*—could miss how, um, *lesbianesquely* she played the part of a lesbian.

The summer after *Salmonberries* appeared, my lover and I spent a weekend up in a tiny Wisconsin town. Browsing in a dusty little thrift shop, we overheard a conversation between two local women, the store clerk and one of her customers. Both were in their forties and kind of dowdy. They were sorting through a pile of old magazines and reflecting on the sad state of popular music.

"You know who I can't stand?" said the customer. "That Sin-*eed* O'Conner."

"You pronounce it Shin-NAY-add, dear," said the clerk. "My son keeps correcting me. But oh, I agree with you. Who does she think she is?" This was long before Sinead denounced the pope on *Saturday Night Live*. As they went on, I gathered that neither of them had ever heard her sing. They were simply outraged by her shaved head.

"Now, I do like that Katie Lang," said the clerk. "That girl has got *such* a good voice. But there's something, oh I don't know, kind of goofy about her."

Salmonberries had obviously not played at the local art cinema. There was no local art cinema. It was a twenty-mile drive even to see *Diehard 2*.

"Yes," said the other. "I just wish she'd let her hair grow out and wear some pretty dresses. If she did that I think she'd probably look beautiful."

As the two women clucked over how beautiful "Katie" would look with the proper feminine coiffure and outfit, my girlfriend and I looked up at each other over the old lamps and dented teapots and flashed each other a Look, smiling.

You know That Look. The 'In-the-Know' Look. When straight people don't have a clue, and a look flashes between you and another gay person, a secret bond of amusement over their ignorant heterocentrism.

Not an entirely nice thing to do, perhaps. Okay, it's maybe even a little smug. But it provides a smattering of compensation for the pain of our everyday social ostracism and invisibility.

I am extremely grateful to those few public figures, like k.d., who have had the courage to come out at this point. I wish I could have been there, in fact, to hear the conversation when those two nice middle-aged ladies in rural Wisconsin found out "that girl" they sensed was somehow "goofy" was the gen-yoo-wine article: a real live dyke who was honest enough to say so on television. And I remember how great it was that, after she came out, she made the most of it—like that classic photo in the barber chair on the cover of *Vanity Fair*.

But I started wondering: What happens in the future to our secret signs and codes and glances when we are accepted by society at large? I like having those moments of unspoken rapport, and I don't want to lose them. As we become more Out, the cultural currency of lesbians and gay men becomes more conscious to straight people—even dowdy ladies in small-town America—and the pleasure of sharing such secret amusements will no longer be possible.

Granted it's a small price to pay for the end of persecution. Still, I think I'll miss getting and giving That Look.

Recently I was daydreaming as I waited for a train in Penn Station in New York. A woman in a business suit caught my eye in the crowd. "Nice t-shirt," she said to me, smiling.

"Oh, thanks," I said, looking down to see what it was I was wearing. It was my Michigan Womyn's Festival t-shirt.

Ah-hah. We smiled and gave each other a Look.

"I was there, two years ago," she said. We started to chat. There were a lot of other people around, but we carried on our lesbian conversation quite openly as we waited for the track gate to open, me with my overstuffed backpack and she with her leather attache case.

Well, I thought, twenty years from now—when, I hope, all the homophobic bullshit and oppression we have to put up with every day of the year will finally really be over, and nobody will assume everybody is straight, and we won't have to worry about being ostracized or attacked, and heaven knows might even be *appreciated* by the mainstream—dykes will still need to give each other Looks like that, just to know who's who.

So, since the New Year is a time for looking back, I want to acknowledge That Look, and tip my hat in nostalgia for the old days when we were all in the underground, and out of necessity had to give each other a silent Look or a secret signal. There are so many places where we still aren't safe, so I'll take a cup of kindness yet for that auld lang sign.

But since the New Year is also a time for looking forward, I want to acknowledge public figures who, just by being honest about themselves, are inspiring countless people they may never even know with the courage to come Out in their own lives. Even when we're "just like everybody else," we won't be just like everybody else. We'll still have our own cultural signals; we'll still need them to recognize each other, in the little towns and in the big city crowds.

Happy New Year!

Getting to Know You

Last year I worked for several months on a publishing project in an office in Chicago's Loop. Three of us—Bernard, Phyllis, and myself—were hired at the same time for the job.

Our boss, Diane, was twenty-five years old. The first time I met her I got dyke vibes, but she was going out with a guy. When I mentioned that I wrote for *Outlines*—the gay and lesbian newspaper—she knew what that was, and then made a point to tell me that her best friend from college was a lesbian.

So we were cool.

I do like to get the sexual identity thing out of the way quickly at a new job, so we can just go on with things around the office, and if there are any homophobes lurking about, it's best to know that, too, right up front. But I'm not a button-wearer, so sometimes it can be a bit awkward to try to work your sexual orientation into the conversation.

It was late Friday afternoon of our first week. We were sitting at our computer stations—the three newcomers, our boss Diane, and a woman named Sue who had been teaching us the ins and outs of the editorial program we were learning. Sue had been working there for a year and was some kind of a computer whiz.

Our stacks of work were done for the week. "Hey," Diane said, "It's Friday afternoon and we're all caught up. We have a few minutes—why don't we play the Question Game."

"The what?"

"It's kind of a tradition in the office, and it's a good way for people to get to know each other a little bit," she said. "Okay, so we need a question."

She thought for a second. "Here we go: If you could be on the cover of any magazine you wanted, which magazine would it be?"

"*Opera News*," said Bernard. Well, that made sense, from the look of him.

"*Rolling Stone*," said Sue the computer maven. Sue was about my age. She was a straight woman, I gathered, but she looked far dykier than I do. She had a tattoo on her earlobe, and listened to heavy metal music all day on headphones while she worked at the computer. She'd already told me that when she was young she was in a biker crowd. Now she goes to raves. She could wear what she wanted and look however she wanted at the job because they really needed her computer expertise.

"*New York Times Book Review*," I said. "And *Lambda Book Report*." If they knew what that was, nobody asked.

"*Wired*. Or maybe *People*," said Diane.

"*Modern Bride*," said Phyllis. Phyllis was a twenty-one-year-old woman who dressed like a drag queen, only much less tastefully. She kept her hair teased up and stiff, and she sported a big diamond engagement ring that she stuck in everyone's face. I'd been working with her less than a week and I already knew the daily itinerary of her upcoming honeymoon.

"Great. See how easy this game is?" said Diane. "Okay, here's another question. If you could date any celebrity you wanted, who would you choose?"

Bernard said he couldn't think of a single celebrity he'd like to date. He was happy with his live-in girlfriend. Who, he said, was studying to be an opera singer.

Oh. Good one.

Sue was next. "Does it have to be somebody who's alive?" she asked sourly.

"I guess not," said Diane.

"Well then, I'd want to date James Dean."

"Who?" asked Phyllis.

We explained as best we could.

My turn. I had given it some serious thought by that time, and there was no doubt in my mind. "I'd like a date with Whoopi Goldberg."

Diane looked at me and scrunched up her mouth thoughtfully.

She nodded. "I could see that."

I didn't know if she meant she could see why I'd want to date Whoopi or she could see dating Whoopi herself.

"What about you?" I asked. "Who would you want to date?"

"Oh, I'd *love* to have a date with Robert DeNiro."

"Robert DeNiro?!" we all echoed.

"Why?" I asked.

"Why?" asked Bernard.

"Yeah, why?" said Sue.

Diane was taken aback by our perplexity. "Because I think he's a great actor—maybe the greatest."

We looked at each other. That sounded reasonable.

"But," she continued, "I'd also really like a date with Jodie Foster."

She smiled.

This went over without a challenge from anybody. I waited for her to say, "...because she's a great director," or "a great actress," or something, but she let it stand at that.

Well, hot damn. I like this game. What a neat way to get to know the people in your office a little bit better!

"What about you, Phyllis?" said Diane.

"Well, you know, I'm *engaged*. But if I wasn't, and I could have a date with a celebrity, I think, um, I'd like to date Robert DeNiro, too."

"Really?" I said.

"You're kidding," said Bernard.

"Oh, come on now Phyllis," said Sue. "Out of *everybody*, you'd want to date Robert DeNiro?! You're just saying that because Diane did."

Actually, I thought maybe Bernard would want to date DeNiro too, but he didn't feel comfortable enough to say so.

"No I'm *not* just saying that. I *love* Robert DeNiro," Phyllis said defensively, "But if it was a guy like around my own *age*, then, um, I think I'd want to date Tom Berringer."

I had no idea who that was. Before I had a chance to ask, she said—so quickly that her words tumbled out over each other: "But if it was a girl, I'd want to date Meg Ryan."

Again, nobody reacted with some remark or some telling body gesture.

And the game ended there, simply because it was time to go home.

"Have a nice weekend!" we all said, out at the elevator. "See you on Monday!"

Maybe Phyllis understood "date Meg Ryan" to be kind of a lunch date or something. Maybe not. Maybe she *would* go out with Meg Ryan—if she wasn't engaged already. Maybe Bernard really is living with a woman. I guess anything can happen these days.

My father was fond of saying "Nothing can stop an idea whose time has come."

You can bet he wasn't thinking of *this* idea. But Holy Moley, if even a terminally heterosexual babe like Phyllis is willing to entertain the notion of dating another woman, the world really must be on the verge of a new sexual revolution.

I realized I had been setting my expectations too low: the goal was for gay men and lesbians to be treated fairly, treated like everyone else. But I had just witnessed three women in an office—including me—suggest having a dream date with another woman, and it caused less of a reaction than the idea of a dream date with Robert DeNiro.

Dyke Victory

It was two a.m. in the dimly-lit lesbian bar in Berlin. I almost felt like I was in a movie, the atmosphere was so strikingly cosmopolitan. Here I was in a German bar that had a French name, chatting with lesbians not only from Berlin but from Canada, Australia, England, the U.S. and Argentina, watching two women I'd recently met in Amsterdam dip dramatically on the dance floor as they tried to tango to old American rock and roll records.

I had been in Berlin for almost two weeks. I'd come at the invitation of Michèle, an ex-Chicagoan who used to work for my newspaper, *Outlines*, and Anja, a German lesbian who was involved in the Green Party and the International Lesbian and Gay Association.

They had taken me to at least one different lesbian gathering place every day, and we still hadn't exhausted them all. The lesbian scene in Berlin was impressively large and diverse. Everywhere we went, I met lesbians—from staunchly-political Green Party women, to women from dyke television, to tough young bar dykes with blue hair, to lesbian expatriates from a number of countries. I'd been to a big lesbian center called the Schoko-Fabrik (a former chocolate factory) that even had a Turkish bath, a big airy women's cafe called the Begine, a yuppified lesbian bar with mirrors and ferns called Dinelo, a no-nonsense non-alcoholic restaurant called Cafe Extra Dry run by 12-Step lesbians, and to a succession of once-a-week women-only soirees in seedy gay bars in different parts of the city.

I'd also strolled by gay bars where so many men crowded the sidewalk that we had to walk in the street. I'd walked along the route of Marlene Dietrich's funeral procession. I'd made a pilgrimage to the place Christopher Isherwood had lived in the early 1930s. And I saw the plaque outside the Nollendorfplatz U-Bahn station dedicated to the gays who had died during the war.

This was my Big Trip to Europe. I'd spent a week in Amsterdam at a feminist conference before coming to Berlin to see Michèle and Anja. Then Leah, a friend of mine from Chicago, had joined us, and now we were all about to leave for a week in Paris, where I was going to cover the International Lesbian and Gay Association's annual conference for *Outlines.*

So tonight was our last foray into the dyke nightlife of Berlin. We'd gone bar hopping with a large group of women we'd joined up with, and finally landed here at Pour Elle. Some of the women in this bar were definitely dykes of the Nineties. But a few wore very demure outfits, and could have stepped out of some old black-and-white Hollywood romance filled with clandestine international intrigue. I half expected to see a glossy-haired Lauren Bacall standing at the bar, gazing over the crowd, exhaling a stream of cigarette smoke as she waited for her Bogart butch.

The bar took up the front third of the space. In the center was the small dance floor. At the back, our group congregated in a comfortable arrangement of sofas and chairs. The women who were dancing the tango had taken ballroom dancing lessons, and they angled expertly in each other's arms as the Shirelles sang "Will You Still Love Me Tomorrow." Leah was dancing, too, with a native Berliner—a very studious-looking, bespectacled woman who, once she got on the dance floor, surprised everyone by shimmying with wild abandon.

"It must be great to be a lesbian journalist," said Nancy, sitting next to me. Nancy had lived in Berlin for two years, but was from Indianapolis. "It sounds so glamorous."

"No, not really," I said, laughing. I'd been a writer for the lesbian and gay press for over ten years, and except for the occasional celebrity interview, the last thing it had been was glamorous. But it was very rewarding, because every week there was another "first"—first openly gay actor, first regular lesbian character on a TV series, first openly gay baseball umpire, first gay- and lesbian-produced television show…

"The scene here in Berlin seems pretty glamorous to me," I

said. "I've been to San Francisco a number of times and even there, there's nothing to compare to the lesbian activities going on here. So many different things. I guess I had this vision of Berlin being really sleazy, corrupt and decadent, from the movies I've seen and the books I've read..."

In fact, both Leah and I had complicated feelings about visiting Germany. Leah is Jewish, the daughter of a rabbi, and both her parents had fled to America as the Nazis advanced through Europe. In my case, my mother's parents were German immigrants, and my grandfather, an atheist and a pacifist, had to leave Germany in 1912, in trouble for drawing political cartoons of Kaiser Wilhelm. As a post-war baby boomer growing up in New York City, to me Germany was my grandparents' far-off, almost-mythological Old Country, a jumble of trolls and frost-giants and Wagnerian singers and delicatessens and beer-mugs and red-cheeked children who wore sandals with their socks on. Only when I got older, I learned about the Nazis and the concentration camps and the war stories of my GI uncle who had landed at Normandy in 1944.

Leah and I were products of the Cold War and the Vietnam War—the age of the Berlin Wall. And now, seemingly miraculously, the Wall was gone. Michèle and Leah and I had walked down the streets where it used to run, dividing West Berlin on one side, East Berlin on the other. Piles of concrete rubble were all that remained of that prison-like barrier people had been shot trying to cross. We climbed up on the rubble and took pictures of each other. We went to the old Checkpoint Charlie, where vendors now sold Soviet army medals as trinkets. We visited the Berlin Wall museum, with documentary photos and an exhibit of huge stacks of the old passports people no longer had to carry.

Berlin did seem to be a very free, open place, despite the occasional news of a mugging by reactionary skinheads. During the past two weeks we'd had literally dozens of interesting, sometimes passionate conversations about politics and history and the lesbian and gay movement in Europe. And walking around Berlin at night, in a city where people didn't carry guns, seemed far safer than walking around Chicago. Still, every time we heard the wailing siren of an ambulance, Leah and I exchanged a troubled glance, because it sounded exactly like the Gestapo sirens from every World War II movie we'd ever seen.

An Australian dyke sat on a sofa a few feet away from where I sat with Nancy and Anja. She had been staring at me for some time, and now she began making waggling motions with her tongue, as if she was the lead singer of Kiss.

"There's a bit of decadent Berlin for you," Nancy said.

I thought the Australian woman was joking, but she continued sticking out her tongue suggestively for minutes, as if she was jiggling an invisible clitoris.

"A strange pick-up technique," I said.

Leah, on a break from her dancing, came and sat on the arm of my sofa. "How's it going?"

"I was just thinking about how the world has shrunk," I said. "Eighty-some years ago, when my grandmother was 14, she got on a German steamer and made a long, arduous journey to the New World all by herself. And here I am, I can get on a plane and eight hours later I'm in her Old Country watching German dykes dancing to "It's My Party and I'll Cry if I Want To."

Leah leaned over and whispered, "I think that woman over there is waggling her tongue at you."

"I know. I'm ignoring her."

"How weird. Think it's a nervous condition?"

"I don't know. Maybe she thinks it's sexy."

"Maybe that's how dykes wave hello in Australia?"

"I don't think so." We both laughed. "What can I say? You attract the cute, smart ones with glasses and I attract the meshuggenahs."

There was a sudden commotion up at the bar. Lots of shouting in German. A woman ran out, and someone else chased after her, yelling.

After a few minutes of hubbub, the story filtered back to us in English: the bartender had been stabbed in the hand by a drunken patron. Some kind of a love quarrel. Someone had chased the attacker, but didn't catch her. Several women had offered to take the bartender to the hospital, but she said she didn't need to go.

Leah and I stared sympathetically at the bartender—a handsome, androgynous woman who looked kind of the way Joel Grey would have looked in *Cabaret* if he had been an Amazon. The injury was apparently not that serious, because she continued swabbing the counter with Nordic stoicism, as if nothing had happened.

About ten minutes after this incident, she came around serving drinks on a small tray. Her right hand was wrapped in a bloody dishrag. "Vould you like anuzzer coke?" she asked me. I glanced at the seeping red stain on the rag around her hand as she held the tray. I smiled as brightly as I could. "Oh, no, not right now, thank you."

"No thanks," said Leah. "Are you okay?"

"Oh, ya," the bartender smiled, and moved on.

"Actually, I'd love a glass of wine, but I think I'll wait till she clots," Leah whispered.

A very large, tall, decidedly femme woman asked Leah to dance, and off they went. The woman wore a big fuzzy cotton-candy pink cashmere sweater. Her blonde hair was pinned up in a neat twist, and she had tight black high heel shoes that must have pinched her feet. I guessed she was about forty. Then Nancy from Indianapolis and I decided to dance, too. On the dance floor, Leah introduced us to her new dancing partner. "This is Heidi."

Heidi nodded. She didn't speak much English, but she danced with dogged determination. I noticed, under the bright lights of the dance floor, that Heidi's pink sweater was studded with white rhinestones that spelled out "Las Vegas" in curly script across the front.

When I was a kid, my grandmother read me the story of Heidi, a little Bavarian girl with pigtails who went to live high on a mountaintop with her grumpy old Grandfather. As I recall, she had to climb up the mountain wearing many layers of sweaters because she didn't have a suitcase. The story never mentioned that Heidi grew up to frequent lesbian bars in Berlin in a pink cashmere sweater—but why not? It amused me to imagine that here was the celebrated Heidi of my childhood storybook in the flesh.

"Look at that," Leah said, gazing at the floor. The dance floor had some smeared red drops of what looked like blood.

"Oh, jeez," said Nancy. "The bartender must have dripped it from her stab wound walking across with the drinks."

Leah pointed to the red smears. "Heidi, ist das blut?"

Heidi shrugged. "Ya," she answered, showing the same nonchalance as the bartender. "Das ist Berlin."

That's Berlin. We continued dancing, to Donna Summer singing "Looking for Some Hot Stuff," but we carefully sidestepped the bright red patches.

Before World War II there were, so I'm told, more than fifty lesbian bars in Berlin. More than *fifty*. They were swept away in the tornado of fascism. The little lesbian places—bars, businesses, organizations, cultural structures that take so much time to build and intertwine to form a social network—were all demolished.

But now they were back.

The women from Amsterdam took to the floor for another round of ballroom dancing—the song had changed to "Stand By Me," which they seemed to think had tango potential—and the rest of us sat down. The Australian tongue-wagger had left the bar. As I watched the tango dancers, I had the sudden chilling feeling that it might have been just like this in 1925—open, optimistic, with the expectation of more freedom and acceptance. With more than fifty bars, lesbians had undoubtedly danced the tango in pre-war Berlin in places like this one, not knowing of the carnage that was coming. These ghostly lesbians danced to older music, to other voices, but the atmosphere might not have been so different. And then a decade later, they found themselves harassed, pursued, arrested, their gathering places closed down. And many were murdered.

How different are we today from them, really? How less vulnerable? Are we any safer from the firestorms of history than they were? As unlikely as it seems, it's not inconceivable—especially with all the rightwing backlash going on in the U.S.—that lesbians and gays might be actively, officially persecuted in America at some time in the future.

As a lesbian writer during the Eighties, I witnessed the tremendous growth of the lesbian and gay community, and watched people who once had been terrified of being "found out" develop the courage to march openly in parades, and live openly in their lives. Despite the decimation of AIDS, and despite the rightwing harrassment and hate-crimes against us, we have gained ground. We have won something. Just for lesbians to get together like this and enjoy each other's company openly is still a victory of sorts—and we mustn't take it for granted.

And the struggle for lesbian and gay rights has become a visible international movement. It would be much harder now to put over the lie that we don't exist, or that we're all somehow defective. I'm not saying it couldn't happen. But we are a legitimate part of a larger, global struggle for humans to treat each other with dignity no matter who they are. Part of a movement of hope and survival. Julia Penelope once compared lesbians to dandelions, because, she said, "every attempt to eradicate us has failed."

What crystallized for me during the time I'd been in Berlin is the obvious fact that lesbian culture has the best chance of flourishing in a free society. Of course there are lesbians capable of committing antisocial, repressive, and even violent acts—like stabbing a bartender in a fit of jealous rage. But every victory over fascism, wherever it occurs, is a victory for us. Every victory over racism is a victory for all of us. Every wall that comes down is a victory for us. Every time a dictatorship is overthrown, it's a victory for us, because the possibility of lesbian love and lesbian relationships increases wherever there is real freedom of thought and action.

"You should come back to Berlin for Christopher Street Day," someone said.

"Or Lesbian Week, in October. It's a whole week of lesbian events..."

Leah and I agreed that we'd love to come back for Lesbian Week if we could sometime. We watched as the bartender, in the middle of the dance floor, wove in and out between the tango dancers. She was bending down and, with her good hand, scrubbing away the smears.

NOTES

Lesbian Connection, mentioned in "The Gadgetry and the Ecstasy" and "Coupledom and Dumber," is a publication "For, By, and About Lesbians," published bimonthy by the Helen Diner Memorial Women's Center, Ambitious Amazons, P.O. Box 811, East Lansing, MI 48826.

The February 21, 1995 issue of the *Weekly World News* contains both the cover story *Loch Ness Monster is Dead!* mentioned in "Dykosaurus" and *You Can Pick Out Gays by Their Fingerprints!* (page 3) quoted in "Testing, Testing..."

Quotes in "If the Shoe Fits" are taken from Walt Disney's *Cinderella*, The Classics video series, Color/76 minutes, copyright 1949 The Walt Disney Company.

The Venus Envy album *I'll Be a Homo For Christmas* mentioned in "Northern Exposure" is available from Ladyslipper Distributors, P.O. Box 3124, Durham, NC 27705, (919) 683-1570. Venus Envy and Dos Fallopia can be contacted by e-mail at tunginchic@aol.com.

Sappho's poetry ("Treasure of the Lost Crocodykes") is available in numerous translations. The introduction to *Sappho: Poems and Fragments*, translated by Josephine Balmer (Brilliance Books, London, 1984) contains a very good discussion of the poet's work from a feminist perspective, and the translations themselves are excellent. The popular translation for many years has been that of Mary Barnard, *Sappho: A New Translation* (University of California Press, Berkeley, 1958), and it is interesting to compare the two. The Loeb Classical Library No. 142, *Greek Lyric I*, translated by D. A. Campbell, contains literal translations of all Sappho's extant poetry in both ancient Greek and English, with sources, and also quotes all extant ancient authors who mention her in their own works.

The quote in "Double Vision" is from *The Ghosts of Versailles*, "A Grand Opera Buffa in Two Acts, Suggested by La Mère coupable of Pierre-Augustin Caron de Beaumarchais." Music by John Corigliano, Libretto by William M. Hoffman. Commissioned by the Metropolitan Opera Company for its 100th Anniversary. The libretto, published in 1991, is available from G. Schirmer, 5 Bellvale Road, Chester, NY 10918.

"Art Dyko" illustrations are from "The Judgment of Paris" (detail) by Lucas Cranach, Munich, Pinakothek; "Gabrielle d'Estrées and one of her sisters" (detail) by School of Fontainbleu, Paris, Louvre; "The Three Graces" (detail) by Peter Paul Rubens, Madrid, Museo del Prado; "The Landing at Marseilles" (detail) by Rubens, Paris, Louvre; and "Helena Fourment" (detail) by Rubens, Munich, Alte Pinakothek.

All quotes cited in "Leon or Leona?" are from *Leonardo da Vinci: A Study in Psychosexuality* by Sigmund Freud, authorized translation by A.A. Brill, Vintage Books, 1947. The illustration is of da Vinci's "The Virgin and St. Anne," also known as "The Holy Family" and "The Virgin and Child with St. Anne." Collection of the Louvre, Paris.

"Going by the Book": The only specific references to homosexuality in the Bible are to be found: in the Hebrew Bible, Leviticus 18.22, 20.13; in the New Testament, Romans 1:26-27; and a passing mention of "effeminates" in the (King James) 1 Corinthians 6:9.

The quote that opens "Experimental Dykology" is taken from the *Comprehensive Textbook of Psychiatry*, edited by Alfred M. Freedman, M.D. and Harold I. Kaplan, M.D., published by the Williams and Wilkins Company, Baltimore, 1967. See Chapter 26, "Personality Disorders. II Sociopathic Type: Antisocial Disorders and Sexual Deviations," Section 26.3, (page 964) "Sexual Deviations II: Homosexuality." That section, including the quote cited, was written by Irving Bieber, M.D.

Rubyfruit Jungle, by Rita Mae Brown, cited in "Experimental Dykology," was first published by Daughters Publishing in 1973, and then by Bantam (New York) in 1977.

The lesbian saga "On the Road" was inspired by the Beat Generation classics *On the Road* (Penguin, New York, 1991, first published by Viking 1957) and *Dr. Sax* (Ballantine, New York, 1959), both by Jack Kerouac, and the poem collections *Howl, Reality Sandwiches,* and *Kaddish* by Allen Ginsberg (see *Allen Ginsberg: Collected Poems 1947-1980*, Harper & Row, New York, 1984).

"Dragonflies Above Our Nation": I do not know which record company originally released Joni Mitchell's song "Woodstock" in the 1960's—I quote the line from memory. But Ms. Mitchell currently records on Reprise Records, a Time Warner Company, 75 Rockefeller Plaza, New York, NY 10019-6908. Pianist Liz Story records on Windham Hill Records, P.O. Box 9388, Stanford, CA 94309.

Acknowledgments

Tracy Baim of Lambda Publications, publisher of Chicago *Outlines* and *Nightlines*, has carried my lesbian humor column, *Lesbomania*, since 1990. Some of the pieces in *Tales from the Dyke Side* originally appeared as *Lesbomania* columns in those publications. Toni Armstrong, Jr. has always been supportive of my writing, and a few of the pieces included here first appeared, in slightly different form, in *Hot Wire: Journal of Women's Music and Culture*, under Toni's editorial direction.

Michèle Bonnarens' faith in my ability to find comic elements in uncomfortable or even unpleasant predicaments has often inspired me to keep looking for them, and thereby sharpened my own sense of humor. I'm delighted that she is contributing her own talents to *Tales from the Dyke Side* as its illustrator.

Paula Walowitz and Marcy J. Hochberg read each of the pieces in this collection while they were still hot off the laser printer. They both offered very helpful editorial suggestions, and gave me a great deal of moral support during the writing process. Paula also thought up the name for the quiz to test someone's level of homophobia (the "Chicago Lesbophobic Indicator Test" or "CLIT") in the "Experimental Dykology" piece. Micki Leventhal gave the manuscript a careful reading in its almost-final form and offered useful feedback at that stage of its completion. Paula Berg has continually afforded insight during conversations about how and why we write what we do. Sylvia B. Stallings and Julie Parson provided a great deal of general encouragement for my work.

Neil Eddinger, Fred Cohen, Dolores Connelly, and Leah Paster all gave advice on specific pieces. Claudia Lamperti, Beth Dingman, and Deborah Dudley of New Victoria Publishers provided useful feedback and have once again demonstrated an almost superwomanly degree of patience in the development of the manuscript.

I owe a special debt of gratitude to my mother, the late Helen Harper, without whom this book might not have been written. She encouraged me to speak up for my own interests when I was a teenager, observing: "The people who do okay in this world are the ones who have a big mouth and who know how to use it." It was good advice, even if I took it in a few directions she didn't foresee. She died just two months after the death of her lifelong friend and next-door neighbor, Mary Cummings. They weren't lesbians, but I hope and expect that they will both be formidable dykes in their next incarnations.

Thanks to those of you who so enthusiastically greeted my first book, *Lesbomania*, so that there could be a second book. And thanks to everyone who in one way or another contributed to the content and flavor of *Tales from the Dyke Side*, including Renata Tebaldi, Laura Nyro, Nina Simone, Om Kalsoum, Edith Piaf, k.d. lang, and Mercedes Sosa, great vocal artists who sang to me through various drafts of these pieces.